FAMILY FAVOURITES

Bargain Box and Nadia Lim

Photography by Tam West

CONTENTS

BARGAIN
BOX
FAST'N
FRESH

LET'S GET STARTED!

WELCOME to the first-ever Bargain Box cookbook. We've enjoyed every moment of bringing this book together and it's our pleasure to serve you these recipes, created straight from the heart!

Bargain Box was born out of the idea of making easy, tasty meals an affordable reality for Kiwis. It's about making the best use of what you've got, getting the kids in the kitchen and adding a bit of variety to your weeknight meals.

An important part of making your Bargain Box meals is involving your little chefs in the cooking process. There are so many benefits to cooking as a family — not only does it produce hearty laughs and happy tummies, getting your kids in the kitchen teaches them lessons for life.

With Nadia Lim at the helm, the Bargain Box team has put together this collection of recipes you can really sink your teeth into. We've gone a little bit further than we normally do each week and added in recipes for irresistible desserts, sauces and dressings — there's even a chapter on ways to make use of those ingredients that are often left over in your pantry or fridge.

If you haven't tried Bargain Box before but fancy giving it a go, head to bargainbox.co.nz and find the option that suits your family size best. You'll find new and exciting recipes popping up every week to inspire and delight.

Thanks to everyone involved in making this book come to life. Enjoy!

THE BARGAIN BOX TEAM

PERFECT PASTA AND NICE RICE

WE RECKON PASTA and rice are some of the most versatile ingredients and are year-round favourites in Bargain Box, even for the fussiest of eaters. We've chosen some of our highest-rating meals that use a variety of fun pasta shapes — fettuccine, penne, spirals, even bowties! There's also a hearty lasagne and a creamy risotto packed with delicious flavours to appeal to the whole family. Perfect for those busy, rushed-off-your-feet weeknights, these go-tos are sure to become crowd pleasers at your place.

UNDER
30 MINS

SERVES 5
PREP TIME 5 minutes
COOK TIME 15 minutes
READY IN 20 minutes

Pea, Ham 'n' Sour Cream Fettuccine

This no-fuss fettuccine can be whipped up super-quick. Just cook the pasta and peas, then ready, steady, eat!

- 450g dried fettuccine pasta (or spaghetti)
- 3½ cups frozen peas
- 360g ham, diced
- 1 cup sour cream or crème fraîche
- juice of ½ lemon
- ¼ cup roughly torn basil leaves, to serve (optional)

BRING a large pot of salted water to the boil. Bring a full kettle to the boil.

1. Add pasta to pot of boiling water, stir and cook for 8–10 minutes, or according to packet instructions, until just tender. Stir pasta a few times while cooking to prevent it sticking together.
2. Place peas in a medium-sized, heat-proof bowl and cover with boiling water. Cover the bowl and leave to cook for about 1–2 minutes, until the peas are bright green and tender. Drain well.
3. Drain cooked pasta then add back to pot along with ham, peas, sour cream or crème fraîche, and lemon juice.
4. Toss everything together and set pot on a low heat until heated through. Season to taste with a little salt (if needed) and freshly ground black pepper.

TO SERVE, divide pea, ham and sour cream fettuccine among serving bowls and garnish with basil (if using).

ENERGY 2218KJ (530kcal)
CARBS 68.2g
PROTEIN 30.4g
FAT 13.8g

FUN FACT

Fettuccine is a thick, flat pasta — it translates to 'little ribbons' in English.

SERVES 6
PREP TIME 15 minutes
COOK TIME 20 minutes
READY IN 30 minutes

Summer Bowtie Pasta

An easy, tasty veggie-packed pasta — perfect served hot or cold.

- 400g dried pasta bowties (or pasta of your choice)
- 1 head broccoli, cut into small florets and stem diced 1cm
- 300g bacon, rind removed, diced 1cm
- 1 red onion, thinly sliced
- 2 cloves garlic, minced (optional)
- 1 courgette, diced 1cm
- 1 capsicum, core and seeds removed, diced 1cm
- 190g basil pesto (store-bought or see page 155)
- ¾ tsp salt
- ½ cup sour cream
- 1 punnet cherry tomatoes, halved
- 1 cup grated cheese, to serve

BRING a large pot of salted water to the boil.

1. Cook pasta in pot of boiling water for 9–11 minutes, or according to packet instructions, until just tender. When pasta has 3 minutes of cooking time remaining, add broccoli and cook until bright green and tender. Drain pasta and broccoli, return to pot, and toss with a little olive oil to prevent sticking.
2. While pasta is cooking, heat a little oil in a large frying pan on a medium heat. Cook bacon for about 5 minutes, until starting to brown. Add onion and garlic (if using) and cook for a further 2–3 minutes, until softened. Add courgette and capsicum and cook for a further 3–4 minutes, until all vegetables are tender.
3. Reduce heat to low-medium and add pesto, salt, sour cream, cherry tomatoes, drained pasta and broccoli. Mix together well until warmed through and season to taste with freshly ground black pepper.

TO SERVE, spoon summer bowtie pasta into bowls and top with grated cheese.

ENERGY 2656KJ (635kcal)
CARBS 51.0g
PROTEIN 29.7g
FAT 34.0g

SEASONAL VARIATION

You could swap the capsicum for mushrooms and the tomatoes for some leafy greens to make this summer pasta dish perfect for winter!

KID
APPROVED

SERVES 6
PREP TIME 20 minutes
COOK TIME 20 minutes
READY IN 40 minutes

Baked Beef Meatballs

With plenty of veggies hidden inside the tasty tomato vegetable sauce, this family fav is nutritious *and* delicious!

Meatballs

600g beef mince
½ cup panko breadcrumbs
1 egg
1 tsp soy sauce
2 tbsp meatball spice mix (see below)
½ brown onion, finely diced
1 clove garlic, minced (optional)
1 tbsp tomato sauce
¾ tsp salt

Meatball spice mix

Mix together 1 tbsp dried rosemary and 1 tbsp dried oregano

Tomato vegetable sauce

½ brown onion, finely diced
1 carrot, grated
3 stalks celery, finely diced
pinch of salt
680ml jar tomato passata
1 cup beef stock
1 tsp sugar
2–3 handfuls baby spinach leaves
¾ cup grated cheese

400g dried spaghetti (or pasta of your choice), to serve

PREHEAT oven and a large casserole dish to 220°C.

1. Combine all meatball ingredients in a large bowl and mix well using clean hands. Scoop out about 2 tablespoons of mixture and roll into a golf-ball-sized ball. Repeat with remaining mixture. Carefully place meatballs into preheated dish, in a single layer, and bake for 10 minutes.
2. While meatballs are baking, prepare the sauce. Heat a little oil in a large frying pan on a medium heat. Cook onion, carrot and celery with salt for 5–6 minutes, until soft. Add tomato passata, stock and sugar and bring to the boil. Simmer on a low-medium heat for 5–6 minutes, until sauce has thickened slightly. Stir through spinach and season to taste with salt and freshly ground black pepper.
3. Remove tray of meatballs from oven and pour sauce over to cover. Sprinkle over cheese. Bake for a further 10 minutes, until cheese is melted and golden.
4. While meatballs are baking, bring a large pot of salted water to the boil. Cook spaghetti for 7–8 minutes, or according to packet instructions, until just tender. Drain and toss with a little olive oil to prevent sticking.

TO SERVE, divide spaghetti among plates and top with baked beef meatballs and tomato vegetable sauce.

ENERGY 2912KJ (696kcal)
CARBS 68.5g
PROTEIN 39.6g
FAT 28.7g

CHANGE IT UP

If your crowd prefers a different shape or style of pasta, simply cook this instead and serve the meatballs on top!

SERVES 5
PREP TIME 15 minutes
COOK TIME 20 minutes
READY IN 30 minutes

Creamy Carbonara

This creamy pasta is best served with a little freshly ground black pepper on top — give it a try!

- 400g dried penne pasta (or pasta of your choice)
- 1 brown onion, finely diced
- 1 clove garlic, minced (optional)
- ½ capsicum, core and seeds removed, thinly sliced
- 125g white button mushrooms, thinly sliced
- 1 courgette, grated
- 200g shaved ham, roughly chopped
- 2 eggs
- 200ml cream
- ½ tsp salt
- 1 cup finely grated Parmesan cheese
- chopped parsley, to serve

BRING a large pot of salted water to the boil.

1. Cook pasta in pot of boiling water for 9–11 minutes, or according to packet instructions, until just tender. Reserve ¾ cup pasta-cooking water, then drain. Return pasta to pot and toss with a little olive oil to prevent sticking. Set aside.
2. While pasta is cooking, heat a little oil in a large frying pan on a medium-high heat. Cook onion and garlic (if using) for 3–4 minutes, until softened. Add capsicum and mushrooms and cook for a further 2–3 minutes, until just tender. Add courgette and ham and cook for 1 minute, until warmed through.
3. While veggies are cooking, whisk eggs in a medium-sized bowl. Add cream, salt and half the Parmesan cheese and mix to combine. Reduce heat to low-medium.
4. Add egg/cream mixture, reserved pasta water and cooked, drained pasta to pan with veggies and ham. Toss well to combine for about 1 minute, until heated through. Season with salt and plenty of freshly ground black pepper.

TO SERVE, divide creamy carbonara among plates and sprinkle over remaining Parmesan cheese and chopped parsley.

ENERGY 2232KJ (533kcal)
CARBS 56.6g
PROTEIN 26.2g
FAT 22.1g

DID YOU KNOW?

Carbonara originated from the Italian city of Rome, home to many more world-famous pasta dishes!

SERVES 6
PREP TIME 15 minutes
COOK TIME 20 minutes
READY IN 30 minutes

Chicken Pesto Pasta

This recipe is one of our Bargain Box customers' most loved meals — we had to share it with you, too!

- 600g boneless, skinless chicken thighs
- 400g dried spiral pasta (or pasta of your choice)
- 1 cup chicken or vegetable stock
- 2 tbsp cornflour
- 1 leek, white and pale green part only, thinly sliced
- 2 tbsp water
- 2–3 handfuls baby spinach leaves
- 250g frozen peas
- ½ cup sour cream
- ¼ cup milk
- 200g basil pesto (store-bought, or see page 155)

BRING a large pot of salted water to the boil.

1. Pat chicken dry with paper towels and season with salt. Heat a little oil in a large frying pan on a high heat. Cook chicken, in batches, for 3–4 minutes each side, until browned (chicken does not have to be cooked through yet). Remove from pan and set aside, covered with foil.
2. While chicken is cooking, cook pasta in pot of boiling water for 9–11 minutes, or according to packet instructions, until just tender.
3. While pasta is cooking, combine stock and cornflour in a small bowl and mix well until smooth.
4. Heat a little oil in same pan used to cook chicken on a medium-high heat. Cook leek for 5–6 minutes, until softened. Add water in final 30 seconds to help leek steam.
5. Roughly chop chicken, reserving the resting juices.
6. Add stock/cornflour mixture, spinach, peas, sour cream, milk, pesto, and chicken and its resting juices to pan with leeks and stir. Bring to a simmer and cook on a medium heat for 2–3 minutes, until chicken is just cooked through.
7. When cooked, drain pasta well and return to pot. Add chicken and sauce to pot with pasta. Toss to combine and season to taste with salt and freshly ground black pepper.

TO SERVE, divide chicken pesto pasta among bowls.

ENERGY 2782KJ (665kcal)
CARBS 51.5g
PROTEIN 31.9g
FAT 36.2g

WHY NOT TRY?

Garnish this dish with some roughly chopped fresh basil leaves for a little added flavour!

MAKE AHEAD

SERVES 6
PREP TIME 20 minutes
COOK TIME 50 minutes
READY IN 65 minutes

Beef Lasagne

A family favourite, this classic lasagne recipe is a favourite with Bargain Box households across NZ — recommended!

Meat sauce

1 brown onion, finely diced
1 carrot, grated
2 stalks celery, finely diced
600g beef mince
2 tbsp dried Italian herbs (see below)
¼ cup tomato paste
400g can chopped tomatoes
1½ cups beef stock
1¼ tbsp soy sauce
1½ tbsp sugar

Dried Italian herbs

Mix together 2 tsp dried oregano, 2 tsp dried thyme, 2 tsp dried marjoram, 1 tsp dried basil and 1 tsp dried rosemary

White sauce

1 egg
200ml cream
¼ cup milk
½ cup finely grated Parmesan cheese

To assemble

6 dried lasagne sheets
½ cup finely grated Parmesan cheese

1 head broccoli, cut into small florets and stem diced 1cm, to serve

ENERGY 2442KJ (584kcal)
CARBS 26.6g
PROTEIN 29.8g
FAT 37.1g

PREHEAT oven to 190°C. Set a medium-sized lasagne dish (measuring about 20cm x 28cm) aside.

1. Heat a little oil in a large frying pan on a high heat. Cook onion, carrot and celery for 3–4 minutes, until softened. Add mince and cook for 5 minutes, breaking up with a wooden spoon as it cooks, until browned.
2. Add dried Italian herbs, tomato paste, canned tomatoes, stock, soy sauce and sugar. Simmer for about 10 minutes, until thickened but still saucy. Season to taste with salt and freshly ground black pepper.
3. While the meat sauce is cooking, prepare the white sauce. In a medium-sized bowl, lightly whisk egg. Add cream, milk and Parmesan cheese and whisk until well combined. Season with salt and freshly ground black pepper. The sauce should be runny.
4. Finely spread about 1 cup of meat sauce over base of lasagne dish. Lay lasagne sheets, in a single layer, to cover snugly, cutting to fit if needed. Spoon over half the remaining meat sauce followed by half the white sauce. Repeat for one more layer (lasagne sheets, meat sauce, white sauce), finishing with white sauce. Sprinkle over Parmesan cheese.
5. Bake for about 30 minutes, until topping is golden. Leave to rest for 5 minutes before serving.
6. When lasagne has about 10 minutes cooking time remaining, bring a medium-sized pot of water to the boil. When lasagne is resting, add broccoli to pot of boiling water and cook for 3–4 minutes, until bright green and tender.

TO SERVE, cut beef lasagne into large squares and place onto plates. Serve broccoli on the side.

COOK'S HINT

You can test if the lasagne sheets are cooked by pushing the pointy end of a knife down through the pasta — the knife should go through easily.

WINTER
WARMER

SERVES 5
PREP TIME 20 minutes
COOK TIME 30 minutes
READY IN 40 minutes

Pea 'n' Pumpkin Risotto with Pesto and Bacon

This easy-to-follow risotto recipe is sure to impress the family. It's a delicious, creamy dish topped with crispy bacon — yum!

Pea and pumpkin risotto

400g pumpkin, peeled and diced 1.5cm
1 tbsp butter
1 brown onion, finely diced
2 cloves garlic, minced
1 tsp dried thyme
½ tsp salt
1½ cups Arborio rice
3½ cups vegetable stock, heated
1½ cups frozen peas
⅓ cup sour cream

Salad

½ iceberg lettuce
2 tomatoes
½ telegraph cucumber
1 tsp vinegar (e.g. cider, balsamic, white wine, red wine)
1 tbsp olive oil

To serve

250g streaky bacon, thinly sliced
4 tbsp basil pesto (store-bought or see page 155)
¼ cup Parmesan cheese, shaved or finely grated

PREHEAT oven to 220°C. Line two oven trays with baking paper.

1. Place bacon on first prepared tray and bake for 15–20 minutes, until crispy. Toss pumpkin with a drizzle of olive oil on second prepared tray and season with salt and freshly ground black pepper. Roast for about 15 minutes, until tender.
2. While pumpkin roasts, melt butter and a little oil in a large, heavy-based lidded pot on a medium heat. Cook onion, garlic, thyme and salt for about 3 minutes, stirring occasionally, until onion is soft. Add rice, stir and continue cooking for a further 1 minute.
3. Add 1 cup stock and cook for 2–3 minutes, stirring often, until almost all stock has been absorbed. Stir in remaining stock. Reduce heat to low-medium, cover and cook for about 15 minutes, stirring often, until rice is tender but grains are still intact.
4. While risotto is cooking, prepare salad. Finely shred lettuce; dice tomatoes; cut cucumber in half lengthways then thinly slice. Set all aside in a medium-sized bowl.
5. Remove lid, add peas to pot with risotto and cook for 2–3 minutes, until peas are bright green and tender and liquid in risotto has absorbed. Stir through sour cream and roasted pumpkin then season to taste with salt and freshly ground black pepper.
6. Just before serving, add vinegar and oil to bowl with salad, toss to combine and season to taste with salt and freshly ground black pepper.

TO SERVE, spoon pea and pumpkin risotto onto plates and sprinkle over crispy bacon. Top with a dollop of pesto and sprinkle with Parmesan cheese. Serve salad on the side.

ENERGY 2422KJ (579kcal)
CARBS 55.4g
PROTEIN 19.9g
FAT 29.7g

PIZZA NIGHT

EVER MET SOMEONE who didn't like pizza? We haven't! Everyone has their favourite tasty topping and with our homemade pizza dough recipe (see page 156) you can even have a go at making your bases from scratch. Once you've tried these combos, pizza is sure to be at the top of your family's favourites list. It's easy to get everyone involved in the chopping and topping, and with a fresh side salad, you've got a nicely balanced meal . . . plus it's light on clean up, too!

FRIDAY
SPECIAL

SERVES 5
PREP TIME 15 minutes
COOK TIME 15 minutes
READY IN 30 minutes

BBQ Bacon Pizzas with Sweetcorn Salad

Sweet and salty make for a taste sensation in this moreish topping combination!

BBQ bacon pizzas

- 2 large (or 3 medium-sized) pizza bases (store-bought or see page 156 to make your own)
- 6 tbsp tomato paste
- 1 tbsp olive oil
- 1½ cups grated cheese
- 225g can pineapple pieces, drained and pieces cut in half (reserve juice)
- 300g bacon, diced 1cm
- 3 spring onions, thinly sliced
- 5 tbsp BBQ sauce

Sweetcorn salad

- 1 cup frozen corn kernels
- 2 tbsp reserved pineapple juice
- pinch of salt
- 1 iceberg lettuce
- 1 tomato
- 1 carrot
- 1 spring onion

PREHEAT oven to 220°C. Preheat two oven trays.

1. Place pizza bases on a clean, dry bench. Mix tomato paste and olive oil together. Spread 2–3 tablespoons of tomato paste/oil over each base, leaving a bit of an edge for the crust.
2. Sprinkle over cheese, pineapple, bacon and spring onions. Dollop over BBQ sauce.
3. Place pizzas onto preheated trays (use a fish slice to help with this). If using three bases, cut one pizza in half and place one and a half pizzas on each tray. Cook pizzas for about 15 minutes, until bases are crispy and golden. Swap position of trays halfway through cooking so they cook evenly.
4. While pizzas are cooking, prepare the salad. Bring a half-full kettle to the boil. Place corn in a small, heat-proof bowl and pour over boiling water. Leave for 2–3 minutes. Drain, run under the cold tap and drain again.
5. Combine reserved pineapple juice and salt in a medium-sized bowl. Thinly slice lettuce; dice tomato; peel and grate carrot; thinly slice spring onion. Add all to bowl with dressing, along with corn, and toss to combine.
6. Slice each pizza into 6–8 pieces.

TO SERVE, place a few slices of BBQ bacon pizza onto each plate and serve sweetcorn salad on the side.

ENERGY 2891KJ (692kcal)
CARBS 86.7g
PROTEIN 35.1g
FAT 21.9g

FUN FACT

Different forms of pizza have been made across the globe for centuries. One of the most basic pizzas, the Margherita, was first created in 1889 using only tomatoes, mozzarella and basil to represent the Italian flag.

SERVES 5
PREP TIME 20 minutes
COOK TIME 15 minutes
READY IN 30 minutes

Veggie Pizzas with Curly Salad

Homemade pizzas are delicious, and a much healthier alternative to those from most pizza outlets.

Veggie pizzas

- 2 large (or 3 medium-sized) pizza bases (store-bought or see page 156 to make your own)
- 6 tbsp tomato paste
- 1½ cups grated cheese
- 125g white button mushrooms, thinly sliced
- 1 courgette, cut in half lengthways and thinly sliced
- 1 capsicum, core and seeds removed, thinly sliced
- 1 tomato, finely diced
- ¾ red onion, thinly sliced
- 1 tsp mixed herbs (see below)
- 3 tbsp basil pesto (store-bought or see page 155)

Mixed herbs

Mix together ½ tsp dried oregano, ½ tsp dried thyme, ½ tsp dried marjoram, ¼ tsp dried basil and ¼ tsp dried rosemary

Curly salad

- 1 baby cos lettuce
- 1 tomato
- ¼ red onion (optional)
- 1 carrot
- 1 tbsp olive oil
- 1–2 tbsp vinegar (e.g. red wine, white wine, cider)

PREHEAT oven to 220°C. Preheat two oven trays.

1. Place pizza bases on a clean, dry bench. Spread 2–3 tablespoons of tomato paste over each base, leaving a bit of an edge for the crust.
2. Sprinkle cheese evenly over the bases and top with mushrooms, courgette, capsicum, tomato and red onion. Sprinkle over mixed herbs and dollop pesto evenly over topped pizzas. Season with salt and freshly ground black pepper.
3. Place pizzas onto preheated trays (use a fish slice to help with this). If using three bases, cut one pizza in half and place one and a half pizzas on each tray. Place into oven and cook until the bases are crisp and golden around the edges, about 15 minutes. Swap position of trays halfway through cooking so they cook evenly.
4. While pizzas are cooking, prepare the salad. Roughly chop lettuce; dice tomato into 1cm pieces; thinly slice red onion (if using); peel carrot into long, thin ribbons.
5. Combine all salad veggies in a medium-sized bowl along with olive oil and vinegar. Season with salt and freshly ground black pepper and toss to combine.
6. Slice each pizza into 6–8 pieces.

TO SERVE, place a few slices of veggie pizza onto each plate and serve curly salad on the side.

ENERGY 2472KJ (591kcal)
CARBS 45.9g
PROTEIN 27.2g
FAT 32.2

FUN FACT

The largest pizza ever made measured over 37 metres in diameter! It needed 4500kg of flour, 90kg of salt, 1800kg of cheese and 900kg of tomato purée.

SERVES 5
PREP TIME 20 minutes
COOK TIME 15 minutes
READY IN 30 minutes

Cheesy Chicken Pizzas with Avocado Salad

If you feel like adding an extra favourite topping or two, don't be shy — add them on!

Cheesy chicken pizzas

- 2 large (or 3 medium-sized) pizza bases (store-bought or see page 156 to make your own)
- 6 tbsp tomato paste
- 1½ cups grated cheese
- 300g boneless, skinless chicken breast, diced 5mm
- 2 tbsp chicken pizza spice mix (see below)
- 2 spring onions, thinly sliced
- 75g cream cheese
- 1 tomato, finely diced
- 3 tbsp sweet chilli sauce (preferably mild; optional)

Chicken pizza spice mix

Mix together 4 tsp dried oregano, 2 tsp dried basil, 1 tsp garlic powder and 1 tsp smoked paprika

Avocado salad

- ½ telegraph cucumber
- 1 tomato
- 1 avocado
- 2 tbsp olive oil
- 1 tsp vinegar (e.g. white wine, red wine, cider)

PREHEAT oven to 220°C. Preheat two oven trays (you can use pizza stones instead if you have them).

1. Place pizza bases on a clean, dry bench. Spread 2–3 tablespoons of tomato paste over each base, leaving a bit of an edge for the crust. Sprinkle over cheese.
2. Mix chicken and chicken pizza spice mix together in a small bowl. Evenly top pizzas with chicken pieces (ensuring you separate pieces to allow even cooking), spring onion, small dollops of cream cheese and tomato. Season with salt and freshly ground black pepper.
3. Place pizzas onto preheated trays (use a fish slice to help with this). If using three bases, cut one pizza in half and place one and a half pizzas on each tray. Cook pizzas for about 15 minutes, until bases are crispy and golden and chicken is cooked through. Swap position of trays halfway through cooking so they cook evenly.
4. While pizzas are cooking, prepare the salad. Dice cucumber, tomato and avocado into 1cm pieces. Combine all in a medium-sized bowl, along with olive oil and vinegar. Season to taste with salt and freshly ground black pepper and toss to combine.
5. Swirl sweet chilli sauce (if using) over cooked pizzas and slice each pizza into 6–8 pieces.

TO SERVE, place a few slices of pizza onto each plate and serve avocado salad on the side.

ENERGY 2556KJ (611kcal)
CARBS 44.1g
PROTEIN 30.2g
FAT 34.1g

DID YOU KNOW?

Over 5 billion pizzas are sold worldwide each year.

SERVES 5
PREP TIME 20 minutes
COOK TIME 15 minutes
READY IN 30 minutes

Nacho Pizzas

A fun and tasty twist on a classic pizza, this yummy recipe is sure to be a hit with the kids!

Nacho pizzas

- 2 large (or 3 medium-sized) pizza bases (store-bought or see page 156 to make your own)
- 6 tbsp tomato paste
- 1½ cups grated cheese
- 2 tomatoes, cut in half and thinly sliced
- ½ capsicum, core and seeds removed and thinly sliced
- ½ brown onion, thinly sliced
- 300g boneless, skinless chicken breast
- 2 tbsp Mexican spice mix (see below)

Mexican spice mix

Mix together 4 tsp dried oregano, 1 tsp dried basil, 1 tsp garlic powder, 1 tsp smoked paprika and ½ tsp chilli powder

To serve

- 2–3 handfuls baby spinach leaves, thinly sliced
- ½ capsicum, core and seeds removed, finely diced
- ½ cup sour cream
- 3 tbsp sweet chilli sauce (preferably mild; optional)
- 150g corn chips

PREHEAT oven to 220°C. Preheat two oven trays.

1. Place pizza bases on a clean, dry bench. Spread 2-3 tablespoons of tomato paste over each base, leaving a bit of an edge for the crust.
2. Sprinkle cheese evenly over pizza bases, then top with tomatoes, capsicum and onion.
3. Pat chicken dry with paper towels and dice into 5mm pieces. Mix chicken and Mexican spice mix together in a small bowl. Evenly top pizzas with chicken pieces. Season with salt and freshly ground black pepper.
4. Place pizzas onto preheated trays (use a fish slice to help with this). If using three bases, cut one pizza in half and place one and a half pizzas on each tray. Place into oven and cook until the bases are crisp and golden around the edges and chicken is cooked through, about 15 minutes. Swap position of trays halfway to ensure even cooking.
5. Slice each pizza into 6–8 pieces.

TO SERVE, scatter spinach and diced capsicum over pizzas. Evenly divide sour cream between pizzas, placing a dollop in the middle of each pizza. Drizzle over sweet chilli sauce (if using). Dig corn chips into sour cream. Place on table for everyone to help themselves.

COOK'S HINT

Make sure the diced chicken is the last item you put on your pizza, so that it cooks through. If you'd prefer a side salad, you could use the spinach and capsicum, add 1 diced tomato, and dress it with a little olive oil and vinegar.

ENERGY 2437KJ (582kcal)
CARBS 57.2g
PROTEIN 29.7g
FAT 25.4g

SERVES 5
PREP TIME 15 minutes
COOK TIME 15 minutes
READY IN 30 minutes

Greek Lamb Pizzas with Pea and Mint Salad

Take your favourite Greek-inspired flavours on a trip to Italy!

Greek lamb pizzas

2 large (or 3 medium-sized) pizza bases (store-bought or see page 156 to make your own)
6 tbsp tomato paste
300g lamb mince
1 tsp lamb spice mix (see below)
¼ tsp salt
1½ cups grated cheese
1 courgette, thinly sliced
½ capsicum, core and seeds removed, thinly sliced
½ brown onion, thinly sliced
100g feta cheese
½ tsp dried mint

Lamb spice mix

Mix together 1 tsp smoked paprika, 1 tsp ground cumin, ½ tsp ground black pepper, ½ tsp ground coriander, ¼ tsp ground cinnamon, ¼ tsp ground nutmeg, ¼ tsp garlic powder, ⅛ tsp ground cardamom and a small pinch ground cloves

Pea and mint salad

250g frozen peas
½ telegraph cucumber
½ capsicum
½ clove garlic, minced
¼ tsp dried mint
3 tbsp mayo
¾ tsp vinegar (e.g. white wine, red wine)

½ iceberg lettuce, to serve (optional)

ENERGY 2386KJ (570kcal)
CARBS 46.5g
PROTEIN 33.9g
FAT 29.0g

PREHEAT oven to 220°C. Preheat two oven trays. Bring a small pot of water to the boil.

1. Place pizza bases on a clean, dry bench. Spread 2–3 tablespoons of tomato paste over each base, leaving a bit of an edge for the crust.
2. Mix lamb mince, lamb spice mix and salt together in a medium-sized bowl with a wooden spoon. Top bases with grated cheese, courgette, capsicum and onion. Top with teaspoon-sized chunks of lamb mix. Crumble over feta cheese and sprinkle with dried mint. Season with salt and freshly ground black pepper.
3. Place pizzas onto preheated trays (use a fish slice to help with this). If using three bases, cut one pizza in half and place one and a half pizzas on each tray. Cook pizzas for about 15 minutes, until bases are crispy and golden. Swap position of trays halfway through cooking so they cook evenly.
4. While pizzas are cooking, prepare the salad. Cook peas in pot of boiling water for 1 minute, then drain and refresh under cold water. Drain thoroughly and place in a large bowl. Dice cucumber and capsicum into 5mm pieces. Place both in bowl with peas.
5. Combine garlic, mint, mayo and vinegar in a small bowl and add to bowl with salad veggies. Mix to combine and season to taste. Cut lettuce (if using) into quarters and separate leaves.
6. Slice each pizza into 6–8 pieces.

TO SERVE, place a few slices of Greek lamb pizza onto each plate. Layer a few lettuce leaves to use as cups to hold the pea and mint salad.

CHANGE IT UP

Dollop a little natural yoghurt over your pizzas to add a cool, creamy quality to your pizza.

MEXICAN FIESTA

HOLA! With vibrant colours and zingy flavours, Mexican food is fresh and fun. Generally a meat or veggie-based sauce is combined with crisp salad ingredients and then served with rice, nachos or tacos. It's easy to create your own flavour combos so you can have it how you like it. Kids love the chance to build their own dinner and the delicious array of flavours will tempt even the fussiest eaters. Leftovers make a delicious lunch the next day — that's if there are any!

SERVES 6
PREP TIME 15 minutes
COOK TIME 30 minutes
READY IN 40 minutes

Chilli Con Carne

This easy chilli con carne recipe will have you cooking authentic Mexican in no time! It also builds flavour after a day or two, so it's the perfect dish to make in advance.

Rice

2 cups jasmine rice
3 cups water
pinch of salt

Chilli con carne

600g beef mince
1 brown onion, finely diced
2 tbsp chilli spice mix (see below)
pinch of chilli flakes or chilli powder (optional)
1 cup frozen corn kernels
400g can red kidney beans, drained and rinsed
3 tbsp tomato paste
400g can chopped tomatoes
1 carrot, grated
1 cup beef stock
½ cup grated cheese

Chilli spice mix

Mix together 2 tsp smoked paprika, 2 tsp dried oregano, 2 tsp onion powder, 1 tsp ground cumin and 1 tsp ground coriander

To serve

¼ cup sour cream
2 tbsp tomato sauce
½ iceberg lettuce

PREHEAT oven grill to 200°C/high. Set aside a large casserole/baking dish (if you do not have an oven-proof frying pan).

1. Combine all rice ingredients in a medium-sized lidded pot and bring to the boil. As soon as it boils, cover with a tight-fitting lid and reduce to lowest heat to cook for 12 minutes. Turn off heat and leave to steam, still covered, for a further 8 minutes. Do not lift lid during cooking or steaming. When rice has finished steaming, fluff up grains with a fork.
2. Heat a little oil in a large frying pan (preferably oven-proof) on a high heat. Cook beef mince and onion, breaking up mince with a wooden spoon as it cooks, for 7–8 minutes, until browned. Add chilli spice mix and chilli flakes/powder (if using) and cook for a further 1 minute, until fragrant.
3. Add corn, beans, tomato paste, canned tomatoes, carrot and stock to pan. Bring to a simmer then reduce heat to low and simmer, stirring occasionally, for 9–12 minutes, until thickened. Season to taste with salt and freshly ground black pepper.
4. While sauce is simmering, prepare the rest of the meal. In a small bowl, combine sour cream and tomato sauce and set aside. Thinly slice lettuce and place in a serving bowl.
5. Sprinkle cheese over mince and place whole pan under grill for about 6 minutes, until cheese is bubbling and golden. If you don't have an oven-proof frying pan, transfer mixture to an oven-proof dish before adding the cheese.

TO SERVE, place chilli con carne, rice, tomato sour cream and lettuce in the middle of the table for everyone to help themselves.

ENERGY 3098KJ (740kcal)
CARBS 83.5g
PROTEIN 38.0g
FAT 25.7g

WHY NOT TRY?

To turn into beef nachos, simply serve the chilli con carne mixture with your favourite corn chips instead of rice.

SERVES 6
PREP TIME 20 minutes
COOK TIME 20 minutes
READY IN 35 minutes

Chicken Soft Tacos

Tacos are a fun, family-friendly meal! The kids will love constructing their own and picking the fillings.

Chicken filling

1 brown onion, thinly sliced
2 cloves garlic, minced
600g chicken mince
2 tbsp taco spice mix (see below)
½ tsp salt
1 green capsicum, core and seeds removed, thinly sliced
2 tomatoes, diced 1cm
400g can red kidney beans, drained and rinsed
4 tbsp tomato paste
½ cup stock (e.g. chicken, vegetable)
¼ cup water

Taco spice mix

Mix together 2 tsp dried coriander, 2 tsp ground cumin, 1 tsp paprika, 1 tsp black pepper and 1 tsp dried oregano

Avo sweet chilli mayo

1 avocado
2 tbsp mayo
2 tbsp sweet chilli sauce (preferably mild)

To serve

10–12 small white or wholemeal soft tortillas
1 lettuce (e.g. cos, iceberg)
2 tomatoes
1 cup grated cheese

PREHEAT oven to 200°C (if using to warm tortillas).

1. Heat a little oil in a large frying pan on a medium-high heat. Cook onion and garlic for 2–3 minutes, until softened. Add chicken mince, taco spice mix and salt and cook for 4–5 minutes, until chicken is browned. Add capsicum and cook for a further 2 minutes.
2. Add tomatoes, beans, tomato paste, stock and water. Bring to a simmer, reduce heat to medium and cook for 8–10 minutes, until liquid has reduced and thickened.
3. To warm your tortillas in the oven, divide into two stacks and wrap in foil. Place in oven to warm through for 10–15 minutes. Alternatively, place tortillas on a plate, covered in cling film, and warm in microwave for about 90 seconds on high just before serving.
4. Mash avocado in a small bowl with mayo and sweet chilli sauce. Season to taste with salt and freshly ground black pepper. Set aside.
5. Thinly slice lettuce and dice tomatoes into 1cm pieces. Place lettuce, grated cheese and tomatoes on a large serving plate. Place tortillas on a serving plate.

TO SERVE, place all ingredients in the centre of the table for everyone to help themselves. To make a chicken soft taco, place a tortilla on a plate, spoon over some chicken filling and top with cheese. Scatter over lettuce and tomatoes. Dollop with avo sweet chilli mayo and fold.

ENERGY 2724KJ (652kcal)
CARBS 53.0g
PROTEIN 38.2g
FAT 28.6g

DID YOU KNOW?

Americans consume over 4 billion tacos every year.

KID
APPROVED

SERVES 6
PREP TIME 20 minutes
COOK TIME 20 minutes
READY IN 35 minutes

Beef Soft Tacos

A little like a Sloppy Joe, we reckon the kids will love the saucy filling in these tasty beef tacos!

Beef filling

1 brown onion, thinly sliced
2 cloves garlic, minced
600g beef mince
2 tbsp taco spice mix (see page 39)
½ tsp salt
1 capsicum, core and seeds removed, thinly sliced
1½ tomatoes, diced 1cm
400g can red kidney beans, drained and rinsed
½ cup tomato paste
½ cup stock (e.g. chicken, vegetable)
¼ cup water

Avo sweet chilli mayo

1 avocado
2 tbsp mayo
2 tbsp sweet chilli sauce (preferably mild)

To serve

10–12 small white or wholemeal soft tortillas
1 cos lettuce
1½ tomatoes
1 cup grated cheese

PREHEAT oven to 200°C (if using to warm tortillas).

1. Heat a little oil in a large frying pan on a medium-high heat. Cook onion and garlic for 2–3 minutes, until softened. Add beef mince, taco spice mix and salt and cook for 4–5 minutes, until meat is browned. Add capsicum and cook for a further 2 minutes.
2. Add tomatoes, beans, tomato paste, stock and water. Bring to a simmer, reduce heat to medium and cook for 8–10 minutes, until liquid has reduced and thickened.
3. To warm your tortillas in the oven, divide into two stacks and wrap in foil. Place in oven to warm through for 10–15 minutes. Alternatively, place tortillas on a plate, covered in cling film, and warm in microwave for about 90 seconds on high just before serving.
4. In a small bowl, mash avocado. Mix in mayo and sweet chilli sauce and season to taste with salt and freshly ground black pepper.
5. Thinly slice cos lettuce and dice tomatoes into 1cm pieces. Place lettuce, cheese and tomatoes on a large serving plate. Place tortillas on a serving plate.

TO SERVE, place all ingredients in the centre of the table for everyone to help themselves. To make a beef soft taco, place a tortilla on a plate, spoon over some beef filling and top with cheese. Scatter over lettuce and tomato. Dollop with avo sweet chilli mayo and fold.

ENERGY 3004KJ (718kcal)
CARBS 45.6g
PROTEIN 33.1g
FAT 34.5g

TIME-SAVER

Warm the tortillas in a microwave if you're short on time.

CATCH OF
THE DAY

SERVES 6
PREP TIME 20 minutes
COOK TIME 20 minutes
READY IN 35 minutes

Fish filling

1 brown onion, thinly sliced
2 cloves garlic, minced
2 tbsp taco spice mix (see page 39)
½ tsp salt
1 green capsicum, core and seeds removed, thinly sliced
2 tomatoes, diced 1cm
400g can red kidney beans, drained and rinsed
4 tbsp tomato paste
½ cup vegetable stock
¼ cup water
600g boneless, skinless white fish fillets
¼ cup flour

Avocado mayo

1 avocado
2 tbsp mayo

To serve

10–12 small white or wholemeal soft tortillas
½–1 lettuce (e.g. cos, iceberg)
½ red onion (optional)
2 tomatoes
¾ cup grated cheese
4 tbsp sweet chilli sauce (preferably mild; optional)
4 tbsp sour cream

ENERGY 2618KJ (626kcal)
CARBS 60.6g
PROTEIN 36.0g
FAT 23.4g

Fish Soft Tacos

Fish tacos are a fun way to get the kids involved in creating their own meals, and are also a good way to get fussier eaters to enjoy this healthy protein!

PREHEAT oven to 200°C (if using to warm tortillas).

1. Heat a little oil in large frying pan on a medium-high heat. Cook onion and garlic for 2–3 minutes, until softened. Add taco spice mix and salt and cook for 1 minute, until fragrant. Add capsicum and cook for a further 2 minutes.
2. Add tomatoes, beans, tomato paste, stock and water. Bring to a simmer, reduce heat to low-medium and cook for about 8 minutes, until liquid has reduced and thickened. Set aside.
3. To warm your tortillas in the oven, divide into two stacks and wrap in foil. Place in oven to warm through for 10–15 minutes. To warm your tortillas in the microwave, place on a plate, cover in cling film and heat in microwave on high for about 90 seconds just before serving.
4. In a small bowl, mash avocado with mayo and season to taste with salt and freshly ground black pepper. Thinly slice lettuce and red onion (if using) and dice tomatoes into 1cm pieces. Place lettuce, red onion (if using), tomatoes and cheese on a large serving plate. Place tortillas on a serving plate.
5. Pat fish dry with paper towels, and season with salt. Place flour in a large bowl. Cut fish fillets into 3–4cm pieces and coat in the flour, shaking off excess.
6. Heat a little oil in a large frying pan (preferably non-stick) on a high heat. Cook fish, in batches, for 1–2 minutes each side, or until just cooked through.

TO SERVE, place all ingredients in the centre of the table for everyone to help themselves. To make a fish soft taco, place a tortilla on a plate, spoon over some fish and filling and top with cheese and sweet chilli sauce (if using). Scatter over lettuce, tomatoes and red onion (if using). Dollop with avocado mayo and sour cream and fold.

SERVES 5
PREP TIME 20 minutes
COOK TIME 20 minutes
READY IN 35 minutes

Veggie Soft Tacos

These Mexican-inspired veggie tacos are super quick and easy but full of flavour. Feel free to add any extra salad items you like.

Veggie filling

- 1 brown onion, thinly sliced
- 2 cloves garlic, minced (optional)
- 2 tbsp taco spice mix (see page 39)
- ½ tsp salt
- 1 capsicum, core and seeds removed, diced 1cm
- 400g can chopped tomatoes
- 400g can black beans, drained and rinsed
- 400g can red kidney beans, drained and rinsed
- ½ cup tomato paste
- ½ cup vegetable stock
- ½ cup water

Sweet chilli sour cream

- ½ cup sour cream
- 1–2 tbsp sweet chilli sauce (preferably mild)

To serve

- 10 small white or wholemeal soft tortillas
- 1 cos lettuce
- 2 tomatoes
- 1 cup grated cheese

PREHEAT oven to 200°C (if using to warm tortillas).

1. Heat a little oil in large frying pan on medium-high heat. Cook onion and garlic (if using) for 2–3 minutes, until softened. Add taco spice mix and salt and cook, stirring constantly, for about 30 seconds, until fragrant. Add capsicum and cook for a further 2 minutes.
2. Add canned tomatoes, black beans, kidney beans, tomato paste, stock and water. Bring to a simmer, reduce heat to low and cook for 8–10 minutes, stirring occasionally, until liquid has reduced and thickened. Season to taste with salt and freshly ground black pepper.
3. While veggie filling is cooking, divide tortillas into two stacks and wrap in foil. Place into oven to warm through for 10–15 minutes. Alternatively, place tortillas on a plate, cover in cling film and warm in microwave on high for about 90 seconds just before serving.
4. In a small bowl, mix sour cream with sweet chilli sauce and season to taste with salt and freshly ground black pepper.
5. Thinly slice cos lettuce and dice tomatoes into 1cm pieces. Place lettuce, tomatoes and cheese on a large serving plate. Place tortillas on a serving plate.

TO SERVE, place all ingredients in the centre of the table for everyone to help themselves. To make a veggie soft taco, place a tortilla on a plate, spoon over some veggie filling and top with cheese. Scatter over cos lettuce and tomato. Dollop with sweet chilli sour cream and fold.

ENERGY 2500KJ (598kcal)
CARBS 76.4g
PROTEIN 27.8g
FAT 16.1g

WHY NOT TRY?

If you like your veggie filling slightly spicier, try adding a pinch of chilli flakes or cayenne pepper to the taco spice mix. If you can't get a cos lettuce, half an iceberg lettuce will also work well.

SERVES 4
PREP TIME 15 minutes
COOK TIME 25 minutes
READY IN 30 minutes

Veggie Nachos

Packed with hidden veggies, these nutritious nachos are sure to put a sombrero-sized smile on everyone's face!

Veggie bean sauce

1 brown onion, finely diced
1 leek, white and pale green part only, cut in half lengthways and thinly sliced
1 carrot, grated
1½ tbsp nacho spice mix (see below)
½ cup water
400g can chopped tomatoes
420g can mild chilli beans
1 tbsp soy sauce
250g frozen corn kernels
1 cup grated cheese

Nacho spice mix

Mix together 1½ tsp ground cumin, 1½ tsp ground coriander, 1½ tsp powdered vegetable stock and 1½ tsp cocoa powder

Salad

½ iceberg lettuce
½ telegraph cucumber
1 capsicum

To serve

200g corn chips
½ cup sour cream

PREHEAT oven grill to 200°C/high. Set aside a large casserole/baking dish (if you do not have an oven-proof frying pan).

1. Heat a little oil in a large frying pan (preferably oven-proof) on a medium heat. Cook onion, leek and carrot for 5–6 minutes, stirring occasionally, until starting to soften. Stir through nacho spice mix and cook for a further 1 minute, until fragrant.
2. Stir through water, canned tomatoes, chilli beans, soy sauce and corn. Simmer for about 5 minutes, until sauce has thickened slightly. Season to taste with salt and freshly ground black pepper.
3. Sprinkle over cheese and grill for 2–3 minutes, until cheese is melted. If you don't have an oven-proof frying pan, transfer mixture to an oven-proof dish before adding the cheese.
4. While veggie bean sauce is grilling, prepare the salad. Thinly slice lettuce; roughly dice cucumber; remove core and seeds from capsicum and roughly dice. Place all in a bowl with a little olive oil and season with salt and freshly ground black pepper.

TO SERVE, place veggie bean sauce, corn chips, sour cream and salad in the middle of the table for everyone to help themselves.

ENERGY 2884KJ (689kcal)
CARBS 72.6g
PROTEIN 23.6g
FAT 31.7g

FUN FACT

Red kidney beans are packed full of protein making this veggie meal perfect for growing kids.

BURGERS 'N' MORE

BURGERS ARE A CROWD-PLEASER all year round. Juicy patties can be prepped ahead of time, a great midweek option when you want a quick 'n' easy meal. Try switching up the flavours to suit your own tastes, or try new spice mixes and accompaniments for a bit of extra variety. Mince is such a versatile ingredient that we couldn't resist adding some recipes for meatballs, rissoles and lamb koftas to this section, each flavoured with a different combo of lively herbs and spices.

SERVES 6
PREP TIME 20 minutes
COOK TIME 30 minutes
READY IN 35 minutes

Chicken Burgers with Roasties

When the evenings are warmer, you can cook the chicken on the barbecue.

Roasties

600g potatoes, scrubbed and diced 2–3cm
1 tsp dried mixed herbs (optional)

Chicken

600g boneless, skinless chicken breasts
1 tbsp chicken spice mix (see below)

Chicken spice mix

Mix together 1½ tsp mustard powder, 1½ tsp salt, 1 tsp brown sugar, 1 tsp garlic powder, 1 tsp dried tarragon, ¼ tsp ground white pepper and ¼ tsp ground turmeric

Slaw

¼ head cabbage
½ iceberg lettuce
2 carrots
¼ cup mayo

To serve

6 burger buns
4–6 tbsp mayo (optional)
tomato sauce (optional)

ENERGY 2106KJ (504kcal)
CARBS 53.6g
PROTEIN 31.3g
FAT 16.9g

PREHEAT oven to 220°C. Line two oven trays with baking paper. Preheat barbecue hot plate to medium-high (if using to cook chicken).

1. Toss potatoes with a little oil and dried mixed herbs (if using) on first prepared tray. Season with salt and freshly ground black pepper and roast for 25–30 minutes, until tender.
2. While roasties are cooking, pat chicken dry with paper towels and cut into steaks. To do this, place your hand flat on top of each breast and slice through the middle horizontally to make two thin steaks. Place on a plate with a little oil, sprinkle with chicken spice mix and season with salt and freshly ground black pepper. Use your hands to coat chicken in spice mix and set aside.
3. Thinly slice cabbage until you have 4–5 cups worth; thinly slice lettuce; grate carrots. Place all in a large bowl with mayo and toss well to coat. Season with salt and freshly ground black pepper.
4. Heat a little oil in a large frying pan on a medium-high heat. Cook chicken for 2–3 minutes each side (depending on thickness), until just cooked through. Alternatively, cook on barbecue. Set aside, covered in foil, to rest for 2–3 minutes.
5. While chicken rests, cut burger buns in half horizontally and place, closed, on second prepared tray. Toast in oven for 5 minutes, until warmed through. Alternatively, toast, cut-side-down, on barbecue for about 30 seconds.

TO SERVE, fill burger buns with chicken and slaw. Drizzle over a little mayo and tomato sauce (if using). Serve roasties and any extra slaw on the side.

FUN FACT

Our American friends eat the most burgers in the world — 50 billion a year. This is enough to circle the planet 32 times!

CROWD
PLEASER

SERVES 6
PREP TIME 20 minutes
COOK TIME 30 minutes
READY IN 35 minutes

Pork 'n' Apple Burgers with Carrot Chips

Shake up your burger repertoire with this tasty pork and apple patty recipe.

Carrot chips

4 carrots, cut into approx. 5cm x 1cm sticks

Pork 'n' apple patties

1 spring onion, very finely chopped
1 egg
1 cup panko breadcrumbs
600g pork mince
1 tbsp pork spice mix (see below)
1 apple, grated
1 tsp mustard (e.g. wholegrain, Dijon)
½ tsp salt

Pork spice mix

Mix together 1 tsp garlic powder, 1 tsp onion powder, ½ tsp dried mint and ½ tsp dried parsley

To serve

2 tomatoes
6 burger buns
butter (optional)
¼ cup mayo
2–3 handfuls baby spinach leaves
¼ cup relish or tomato sauce (optional)

ENERGY 2111KJ (505kcal)
CARBS 49.0g
PROTEIN 30.1g
FAT 19.7g

PREHEAT oven to 230°C. Line two oven trays with baking paper. Preheat barbecue hot plate to medium (if using to cook burger patties).

1. Toss carrots with a little oil on first prepared tray. Season with salt and freshly ground black pepper. Roast for about 30 minutes, until golden and cooked through. Turn once during cooking.
2. Place all pork 'n' apple patty ingredients in a large bowl and mix well using clean hands. Using a ½ cup measure, shape mixture into about 8 even-sized balls then flatten into large patties, about 1cm thick and slightly larger in diameter than buns.
3. Heat a little oil in a large frying pan on a medium heat. Cook patties, in two batches, for about 3–4 minutes each side, until browned and cooked through. Turn down heat if beginning to burn. Wipe out pan between batches if necessary. Alternatively, cook patties on barbecue hot plate following the same method. Set aside, covered to keep warm, while you cook the second batch.
4. Thinly slice tomatoes. Cut buns in half horizontally and spread with butter (if using). Place buns, closed, on second prepared tray. Place tray in oven (on rack below carrots) to toast buns for about 4 minutes.

TO SERVE, place a spoonful of mayo on the base of each bun, then top with baby spinach leaves, tomato and a spoonful of relish or tomato sauce (if using). Top with a pork 'n' apple patty, finishing with top half of bun. Serve carrot chips and any remaining spinach, tomato or patties on the side.

COOK'S HINT

You'll have more patties than you may need but any that are left over make a great lunch the next day.

SERVES 6
PREP TIME 15 minutes
COOK TIME 25 minutes
READY IN 30 minutes

Beef Burgers with Carrot Chips

Nothing beats a classic beef burger — especially with our favourite, tried-and-tested beef patties!

Carrot chips

4 carrots, cut into approx. 5cm x 1cm sticks

Beef patties

600g beef mince
2 tbsp burger spice mix (see below)
1 tbsp soy sauce
½ brown onion, finely diced
1 egg
¼ tsp salt
1 cup fine breadcrumbs

Burger spice mix

Mix together 2 tsp dried oregano, 2 tsp dried rosemary, 2 tsp garlic powder and 2 tsp onion powder

To serve

2 tomatoes
½ lettuce
½ brown onion (optional)
6 burger buns
butter (optional)
¼ cup tomato sauce (optional)
¼ cup mayo

PREHEAT oven to 230°C. Line two oven trays with baking paper. Preheat barbecue hot plate to medium-high (if using to cook burger patties).

1. Toss carrots with a little oil on first prepared tray. Roast for about 20 minutes, until golden and cooked through. Turn once during cooking.
2. Place all beef patty ingredients in a large bowl and mix well using clean hands. Using a ½ cup measure, shape beef mixture into 6 even-sized balls then flatten into large patties, about 5mm thick and slightly larger in diameter than buns.
3. Heat a little oil in a large frying pan on a medium heat. Cook patties, in batches, for about 2 minutes each side, until browned (they do not need to be cooked through yet). Wipe out pan between batches. Transfer to one side of second prepared tray. Alternatively, cook patties on barbecue hot plate for 5–6 minutes each side, until cooked through.
4. Thinly slice tomatoes, lettuce and onion (if using). Cut burger buns in half horizontally and spread with butter (if using). Place, closed, on tray with patties. Place tray in oven (on rack below carrots) for about 4 minutes to toast buns and finish cooking patties.

TO SERVE, place a beef patty on bun bottoms, and top with tomato sauce and onion (if using), tomato, lettuce and mayo. Finish with top half of bun. Serve carrot chips and any remaining salad ingredients on the side.

ENERGY 2210KJ (528kcal)
CARBS 47.2g
PROTEIN 29.6g
FAT 23.5g

WHY NOT TRY?

The hamburger is the original burger. It was brought to the US by German immigrants, and has become popular all around the world.

SERVES 6
PREP TIME 15 minutes
COOK TIME 30 minutes
READY IN 35 minutes

Lamb 'n' Lentil Burgers with Veggie Chips

This burger is packed with nutritious ingredients and made lighter by using pita breads, hummus and lentils — yum!

Parsnip and carrot chips

2 parsnips, cut into approx. 5cm x 1.5cm sticks
2 carrots, cut into approx. 5cm x 1.5cm sticks

Lamb patties

½ brown onion, finely diced
500g lamb mince
400g can brown lentils, drained and rinsed
2 tbsp lamb burger spice mix (see below)
2 tbsp soy sauce
¼ tsp salt
1 egg
1 cup fine breadcrumbs

Lamb burger spice mix

Mix together 1½ tsp ground cumin, 1½ tsp ground coriander, 1½ tsp garlic powder, 1½ tsp onion powder, ¾ tsp dried mint and ¾ tsp dried rosemary

To serve

100g hummus (store-bought)
2 tbsp mayo
1 tbsp sweet chilli sauce (preferably mild; optional)
8 small pita breads
2 tomatoes
1 cos lettuce
butter (optional)

ENERGY 2237KJ (535kcal)
CARBS 57.8g
PROTEIN 32.0g
FAT 18.2g

PREHEAT oven to 220°C. Line two oven trays with baking paper. Preheat barbecue hot plate to medium-high (if using to cook burger patties).

1. Toss parsnips and carrots with a little oil on first prepared tray. Season with salt and freshly ground black pepper and cook for 25–30 minutes, until golden and cooked through. Turn once during cooking.
2. Place all lamb patty ingredients in a large bowl and use clean hands to mix well. Using a ½ cup measure, shape lamb mixture into 8 even-sized balls, then flatten into large patties, 5mm–1cm thick and slightly larger in diameter than pita breads.
3. Heat a little oil in a large frying pan on medium-high heat. Cook patties, in batches, for 3–5 minutes each side until browned and cooked through. Alternatively, cook lamb patties on barbecue following same method.
4. While patties are cooking, mix together hummus, mayo and sweet chilli sauce (if using) in a small bowl and set aside.
5. Cut pita breads in half horizontally and place, closed, on second prepared tray. When parsnips and carrots have about 4 minutes of cooking time remaining, place tray with pita breads in oven (on rack below parsnips and carrots) to toast. Toast pita breads for 3–4 minutes, until warmed through.
6. While pita breads are toasting, prepare sides. Thinly slice tomatoes and tear up lettuce. Place both on a serving platter.

TO SERVE, spread butter (if using) on each side of pita breads. On the base of each pita bread, place a spoonful of hummus mayo, a lamb patty and some tomato and lettuce. Finish with another spoonful of hummus mayo and a little extra sweet chilli sauce (if desired), and top with other half of pita bread. Serve parsnip and carrot chips and any remaining lettuce and tomato on the side.

SERVES 6
PREP TIME 20 minutes
COOK TIME 30 minutes
READY IN 40 minutes

Fish Burgers with Kumara and Carrot Chips

This recipe for a kiwi classic coats the fish with an old-fashioned eggy batter — just like at the fish 'n' chip shop!

Kumara and carrot chips

400g red kumara, scrubbed and cut into approx. 5cm x 1cm sticks
2 carrots, cut into approx. 5cm x 1cm sticks
2 tbsp fish 'n' chips spice mix (see below)

Lemon mayo

½ cup mayo
zest of ½ lemon
1 tbsp lemon juice

Fish

600g boneless, skinless white fish fillets
½ cup flour, seasoned with ½ tsp salt
1½ tbsp fish 'n' chips spice mix (see below)
1 egg
1½ tbsp water

Fish 'n' chips spice mix

Mix together 4 tsp garlic powder, 4 tsp onion powder, 2 tsp paprika, 2 tsp dried parsley and 1 tsp ground black pepper

To serve

½ iceberg lettuce
2 tomatoes
6 burger buns
2 tbsp butter (optional)

ENERGY 2487KJ (594kcal)
CARBS 62.2g
PROTEIN 25.8g
FAT 25.7g

PREHEAT oven to 220°C. Line two oven trays with baking paper.

1. Toss kumara and carrots with a little oil and first measure of fish 'n' chips spice mix on first prepared tray. Season with salt and freshly ground black pepper and bake for 25–30 minutes, until golden and cooked through.
2. While chips cook, prepare the rest of the meal. In a small bowl, mix together mayo, lemon zest and lemon juice. Season to taste with freshly ground black pepper. Set aside.
3. Cut lettuce into quarters and separate leaves. Thinly slice tomatoes. Place both on a large serving plate.
4. Pat fish dry with paper towels. Cut fillets in half or, if large, cut into quarters (to fit inside burger buns). Place seasoned flour in a bowl with second measure of fish 'n' chips spice mix. Whisk egg with water in a second bowl. When kumara and carrots have 15 minutes of cooking time remaining, heat a little oil in a large frying pan on a medium-high heat.
5. Coat each piece of fish first in flour mix, then egg mix, shaking off excess as you go and ensuring both sides are coated. Add straight to pan from the bowl and cook, in batches, for 1–2 minutes each side (depending on thickness), until just cooked through. Place on paper towels to drain slightly before serving and season with a pinch of salt.
6. While fish is cooking, cut burger buns in half horizontally and spread with butter (if using). Place, closed, on second prepared tray and toast in oven for 5 minutes, until warmed through.

TO SERVE, spread bases of buns with lemon mayo, top with a few pieces of lettuce and tomato, place fish on top, and top with the lid of bun. Serve kumara and carrot chips and any extra lettuce and tomato on the side.

SERVES 6
PREP TIME 10 minutes
COOK TIME 35 minutes
READY IN 45 minutes

Use a 1.2kg mixture of some/all of the below:

- carrots, ends trimmed, quartered lengthways then cut into 2cm-thick chips
- parsnips, ends trimmed, quartered lengthways then cut into 2cm-thick chips
- beetroot, ends trimmed, peeled then cut into 1cm-thick chips
- kumara (e.g. red, orange, gold), scrubbed then cut into 1cm-thick chips
- potatoes, scrubbed then cut into 1cm-thick chips

Veggie Chips

PREHEAT oven to 220°C. Line one or two oven trays with baking paper.

1. Place veggies onto prepared tray(s), toss with a little olive oil and season well with salt and freshly ground black pepper. Ideally, arrange in a single layer on each tray.
2. Bake for 30–35 minutes, until tender and golden. Turn once halfway (and swap trays if needed), to ensure even cooking.

SERVE with your favourite tomato sauce or other dipping sauce, as a side to burgers, as a snack or with some fish or other protein.

The nutritional information for these chips is highly variable depending on the veggies used.

SEASONAL VARIATION

There are plenty of veggies you can bake into chips. If you've given all the suggestions here a go, try roasting capsicum, courgette or pumpkin sticks. Green beans or taro are great, too. Don't forget to turn or toss your chips halfway through the cook time to ensure even cooking!

KID
APPROVED

SERVES 4
PREP TIME 15 minutes
COOK TIME 20 minutes
READY IN 30 minutes

Lamb Kofta Pita Pockets

Making your own tomato sauce is easy, and this recipe makes plenty of it — be sure to sauce up your pita pockets!

Tomato sauce

½ brown onion, finely diced
1 tbsp tomato paste
400g can chopped tomatoes
2 tbsp sugar
¼ tsp salt
½ tsp vinegar (e.g. white wine, red wine, cider)

Lamb kofta

600g lamb mince
1 tsp salt
½ tsp freshly ground black pepper
½ brown onion, finely diced or grated
2 cloves garlic, minced
1 tbsp Turkish spice rub (see below)
1½ tbsp cornflour
1 egg

Turkish spice rub

Mix together 1 tsp ground cumin, 1 tsp ground coriander, ½ tsp ground allspice, ½ tsp ground fennel seeds and ¼ tsp ground cinnamon

To serve

¼ head cabbage
1 carrot
1 apple
¼ cup mayo
8 small (or 4 large) pita breads

ENERGY 2833KJ (678kcal)
CARBS 60.2g
PROTEIN 48.4g
FAT 26.4g

PREHEAT oven to 220°C and line two oven trays with baking paper or preheat barbecue hot plate to medium (if using to cook lamb kofta).

1. Heat a little oil in a medium-sized pot on a low-medium heat. Cook onion for 4–5 minutes, until softened. Stir in tomato paste, canned tomatoes, sugar and salt. Bring to a simmer, reduce heat to low and simmer for a further 6–8 minutes, until thickened slightly. Stir through vinegar and season with freshly ground black pepper. Set aside.
2. In a large bowl, using clean hands, mix all lamb kofta ingredients together until well combined. Roughly pull away pieces of lamb kofta mixture (about 1 tablespoon per piece), roll into cigar shapes and arrange on first prepared tray. Bake for about 12 minutes, until just cooked through. If using barbecue, roll kofta into balls, flatten, and cook for 2–3 minutes each side, until cooked through.
3. Thinly slice cabbage until you have 2-3 cups worth, and grate carrot and apple. Place in a large bowl with mayo and mix to combine. Season to taste with salt and freshly ground black pepper.
4. Use a sharp knife to cut into each pita bread horizontally to create an opening. Place on second prepared tray and warm in oven for 2–3 minutes, until heated through. If using barbecue, toast for about 30 seconds each side, until warm.

TO SERVE, stuff pita pockets with salad, a few lamb kofta pieces and tomato sauce. Serve extra salad on the side.

FUN FACT

The name kofta comes from the Persian word *kōftan*, meaning 'to pound' or 'to grind'.

SERVES 5
PREP TIME 10 minutes
COOK TIME 20 minutes
READY IN 30 minutes

Moroccan Meatballs with Couscous Salad

Cumin, coriander and turmeric are all popular spices in Moroccan cuisine. Enjoy these fragrant flavours, meatball-style!

Moroccan meatballs

600g beef mince
¾ cup panko breadcrumbs
1½ tbsp Moroccan spice mix (see below)
1 cup grated cheese
1 tbsp soy sauce
1 egg
¼ tsp salt
1 tbsp tomato sauce

Moroccan spice mix

Mix together 2 tsp ground coriander, 2 tsp ground cumin, 2 tsp smoked paprika, 1 tsp garlic powder and ½ tsp ground turmeric

Couscous salad

1 cup boiling water
1 cup couscous
½ tsp salt
1 head broccoli, cut into small florets and stem diced 1cm
½ telegraph cucumber
1 carrot
1 tbsp vinegar (e.g. red wine, white wine, cider)
1–2 tbsp olive oil

To serve

½ cup sour cream
½ tsp Moroccan spice mix (see above; optional)

ENERGY 2864KJ (685kcal)
CARBS 34.8g
PROTEIN 40.4g
FAT 42.6g

PREHEAT oven to 220°C and position oven rack in centre of oven. Lightly grease a large casserole dish (measuring about 25cm x 35cm) and place into oven to preheat. Bring a full kettle to the boil. Bring a small pot of salted water to the boil. Preheat barbecue hot plate to medium-high (if using to cook meatballs).

1. Place all Moroccan meatball ingredients in a large bowl and mix well using clean hands. Roll into golf-ball-sized balls. Carefully place into preheated baking dish in a single layer and bake for 13–15 minutes, until cooked through. Turn oven setting to grill (leaving oven rack in centre of oven) and grill meatballs for 2–3 minutes, until golden. Alternatively, cook on barbecue hot plate for 8–9 minutes, turning often, until cooked through.
2. While meatballs cook, prepare the rest of the meal. In a large, heat-proof bowl, combine boiling water, couscous and salt. Stir, cover and leave to swell for 5 minutes. Fluff up grains with a fork.
3. Prepare veggies. Cook broccoli in pot of boiling water for 3–4 minutes, until bright green and tender. Drain, place under cold, running water to cool and drain again. Quarter cucumber lengthways and dice into 1cm pieces; grate carrot. Stir all veggies through cooked couscous, along with vinegar and olive oil. Season to taste with salt and freshly ground black pepper.
4. In a small bowl, mix sour cream with second measure of Moroccan spice mix (if using).

TO SERVE, divide couscous salad among plates and top with a few Moroccan meatballs. Spoon over sour cream.

DID YOU KNOW?

Turmeric is part of the ginger family. In India, the world's largest producer of turmeric, it is known as the Golden Spice.

SERVES 4
PREP TIME 20 minutes
COOK TIME 15 minutes
READY IN 30 minutes

Greek Lamb Rissoles with Summer Salad

Lamb, cucumber and yoghurt are a classic Greek flavour combo. Give this tasty trio a go in this summery recipe!

Summer salad

1½ cups couscous
½ tsp salt
1½ tbsp summer spice mix (see below)
1½ cups boiling water
250g frozen peas
1 tomato
¼ telegraph cucumber
1 capsicum, core and seeds removed
2–3 handfuls baby spinach leaves
2 tbsp olive oil

Greek lamb rissoles

600g lamb mince
½ brown onion, finely diced
½ tsp salt
1 tbsp summer spice mix (see below)
½ cup fine breadcrumbs

Cucumber yoghurt

150g natural yoghurt
¼ telegraph cucumber
1 tsp sweet chilli sauce (preferably mild)

Summer spice mix

Mix together 2½ tsp ground cumin, 2 tsp ground coriander, 2 tsp dried parsley, 1 tsp onion powder, 1 tsp garlic powder and ½ tsp dried mint

PREHEAT oven to 220°C and line an oven tray with baking paper or preheat barbecue hot plate to medium-high (if using to cook rissoles). Bring a small pot of water to the boil. Bring a full kettle to the boil.

1. In a medium-sized heat-proof bowl, combine couscous, salt, first measure of summer spice mix and boiling water. Stir, cover and leave to swell for 5 minutes, then fluff up grains with a fork. Set aside to cool, stirring occasionally.
2. In a large bowl, using clean hands, mix all Greek lamb rissole ingredients together well. Use clean hands to shape tablespoon-sized amounts of mixture into balls, place on prepared tray and flatten slightly with a fork. Bake for 12–14 minutes, until cooked through and lightly golden. Alternatively, cook on barbecue hot plate for 12–14 minutes, turning regularly to brown on all sides.
3. While rissoles are cooking, prepare remainder of summer salad. Place peas in pot of boiling water and cook for 1–2 minutes, until bright green and tender. Refresh under cold water and drain well.
4. Dice tomato, cucumber and capsicum into 1cm pieces. Roughly chop spinach and place in a large bowl along with other vegetables and cooled couscous. Add olive oil, season to taste with salt and freshly ground black pepper and mix well.
5. Place yoghurt in a small bowl. Grate cucumber into bowl, add sweet chilli sauce, mix to combine and season to taste with salt and freshly ground black pepper.

TO SERVE, spoon summer salad into bowls. Place a few Greek lamb rissoles on top and spoon over cucumber yoghurt. Drizzle over extra sweet chilli sauce (if desired).

COOK'S HINT

Dampen your hands before rolling the rissoles to stop the mixture sticking to your hands.

ENERGY 2468KJ (590kcal)
CARBS 57.9g
PROTEIN 57.9g
FAT 17.9g

ASIAN INSPIRATION

WE LOVE THE WAY Asian ingredients and cooking methods have become infused with our approach to dinners here in New Zealand. Often packed with hidden veggies, these dishes are a great way to introduce healthy ingredients to picky eaters who need a little confidence boost. Adapt and adjust the spice levels to suit younger members of the family or try swapping out rice for noodles with some recipes. You'll find everything from curries to stir-fries in this section, and plenty for little chefs to help out with, too!

SERVES 5
PREP TIME 15 minutes
COOK TIME 25 minutes
READY IN 30 minutes

Beef Satay Stir-Fry

You can use this satay sauce recipe for other proteins such as chicken, or for a vegetarian meal instead.

Rice

2 cups jasmine rice
3 cups water
pinch of salt

Beef

600g beef stir-fry strips (at room temperature)
1 tbsp soy sauce
1 tbsp sesame seeds (optional)

Satay sauce

4 tbsp soy sauce
1 tbsp sweet chilli sauce (preferably mild)
60g peanut butter
½ cup water
½ tsp vinegar (e.g. white, white wine, red wine)

Vegetables

2 carrots
1 courgette
1 capsicum
2 cups thinly sliced cabbage

1 tbsp sesame seeds, to serve (optional)

1. Combine all rice ingredients in a medium-sized lidded pot and bring to the boil. As soon as it boils, cover with a tight-fitting lid and reduce to lowest heat to cook for 12 minutes. Turn off heat and leave to steam, still covered, for a further 8 minutes. Do not lift lid during cooking or steaming. When rice has finished steaming, fluff up grains with a fork.
2. While rice is cooking, prepare the rest of the meal. Pat beef dry with paper towels, place in a medium-sized bowl with soy sauce and sesame seeds (if using) and toss to coat. In a small bowl, whisk all satay sauce ingredients together, until smooth.
3. Cut carrots and courgette in half lengthways and thinly slice. Remove core and seeds from capsicum and thinly slice. Set all aside with sliced cabbage.
4. Heat a little oil in a large frying pan on a high heat. Stir-fry beef, in two batches, for about 1 minute, until browned. Set aside on a plate, covered with foil, to rest. Wipe pan clean with paper towels.
5. Add a little more oil to same pan used to cook beef and stir-fry carrots for about 3 minutes, until just tender. Add courgette, capsicum and cabbage and stir-fry for a further 2 minutes, until vegetables are just cooked. Stir through beef and satay sauce and leave on heat for about 1 minute, until hot and bubbling.

TO SERVE, spoon rice onto plates and top with beef satay stir-fry. Sprinkle over a pinch of sesame seeds (if using).

ENERGY 2475KJ (592kcal)
CARBS 71.3g
PROTEIN 35.9g
FAT 17.7g

FUN FACT

Satay originated on the Indonesian island of Java, and is one of Indonesia's national dishes. Different types of satay are found all over South East Asia as a popular street food.

SERVES 4
PREP TIME 15 minutes
COOK TIME 25 minutes
READY IN 30 minutes

Coconut Chicken

Marinating chicken in coconut cream makes for moist, tasty mouthfuls — go on, try this technique out!

Rice

2 cups jasmine rice
1½ tbsp coconut chicken spice mix (see below)
3 cups water
½ tsp salt

Coconut chicken

600g boneless, skinless chicken thighs
1 tbsp coconut chicken spice mix (see below)
pinch of chilli flakes or chilli powder (optional)
¼ cup coconut cream
½ tsp salt

Coconut chicken spice mix

Mix together 2 tsp curry powder, 2 tsp ground cumin, 2 tsp ground coriander, 1 tsp ground turmeric and ½ tsp ground ginger

Salad

1 carrot
1 capsicum
2–3 handfuls baby spinach leaves
¼ cup coconut cream
¼ cup mayo
1 tbsp lemon juice

1–2 tbsp roughly chopped coriander, leaves and stalks, to serve (optional)

PREHEAT barbecue grill or hot plate to medium-high (if using to cook chicken).

1. Combine all rice ingredients in a medium-sized lidded pot and bring to the boil. As soon as it boils, cover with a tight-fitting lid and reduce to lowest heat to cook for 12 minutes. Turn off heat and leave to steam, still covered, for a further 8 minutes. Do not lift lid during cooking or steaming. When rice has finished steaming, fluff up grains with a fork.
2. While rice is cooking, prepare the coconut chicken. Pat chicken dry with paper towels and place in a medium-sized bowl with coconut chicken spice mix, chilli flakes/powder (if using), coconut cream and salt. Toss to coat and set aside to marinate.
3. Grate carrot; remove core and seeds from capsicum and roughly dice. Place both in a large bowl with baby spinach. In a small bowl, whisk coconut cream, mayo and lemon juice together and set aside.
4. Heat a little oil in a large frying pan on a medium-high heat. Cook chicken for 4–5 minutes on each side, until golden and cooked through. Alternatively, cook chicken on barbecue grill or hot plate for 4–5 minutes each side, until golden and cooked through. Set aside, covered with foil, to rest for 2–3 minutes, then slice.
5. Toss half the dressing through the salad (reserving remainder to serve). Season to taste with salt and freshly ground black pepper.

TO SERVE, spoon rice onto each plate and top with slices of coconut chicken. Serve salad on the side and spoon extra dressing over chicken, as desired. Garnish with coriander (if using).

ENERGY 2411KJ (576kcal)
CARBS 57.2g
PROTEIN 22.7g
FAT 28.7g

SERVES 5
PREP TIME 15 minutes
COOK TIME 25 minutes
READY IN 35 minutes

Chicken Stir-Fry

An easy, filling, go-to meal for weeknights. With classic Asian flavours, this is an easy way to pack veggies into the kids' diet.

Rice

2 cups jasmine rice
3 cups water
pinch of salt

Chicken stir-fry

½ cup flour
1 tsp salt
600g boneless, skinless chicken thighs
1 head broccoli
1 carrot
1 capsicum
2–3 handfuls baby spinach leaves

Soy ginger sauce

3 tbsp soy sauce
1 tbsp finely grated ginger
2–3 tbsp sweet chilli sauce (preferably mild)
½ cup water

1. Combine all rice ingredients in a medium-sized lidded pot and bring to the boil. As soon as it boils, cover with a tight-fitting lid and reduce to lowest heat to cook for 12 minutes. Turn off heat and leave to steam, still covered, for a further 8 minutes. Do not lift lid during cooking or steaming. When rice has finished steaming, fluff up grains with a fork.
2. Combine flour and salt in a small bowl. Pat chicken dry with paper towels and cut into 3cm pieces. Toss in seasoned flour until evenly covered.
3. Heat a little oil in a large frying pan on a medium-high heat. Shake excess flour off chicken and cook, in batches, for 2–3 minutes each side. Reduce heat if browning too quickly and add more oil to pan as required. Remove from pan and set aside, covered, to rest. Reserve flour bowl, including any excess flour, to make sauce.
4. While chicken cooks, prepare veggies. Cut broccoli into medium florets and dice stem into 1cm pieces; dice carrot into 1cm pieces; remove core and seeds from capsicum and finely dice.
5. In a small bowl, combine all soy ginger sauce ingredients with 2 tablespoons of reserved flour from chicken (discard the remainder). Stir well to remove any lumps. Return pan to a medium heat with a little oil. Stir-fry broccoli, carrot and capsicum for 2–3 minutes, until starting to soften.
6. Add spinach and soy ginger sauce. Cook for 1–2 minutes, until spinach has wilted and sauce is starting to thicken. Return chicken and any resting juices to pan and toss to coat.

TO SERVE, spoon rice onto plates and top with chicken stir-fry.

TIME-SAVER

Make sure you have all your veggies chopped before starting cooking, as you don't want to overcook them. The veggies should be tender with a bit of a bite.

ENERGY 2650KJ (633kcal)
CARBS 84.8g
PROTEIN 31.5g
FAT 17.9g

SERVES 4
PREP TIME 15 minutes
COOK TIME 30 minutes
READY IN 35 minutes

Pork Fried Rice

A healthy, veggie-packed take on the classic Chinese takeaway dish.

1½ cups jasmine rice
2¼ cups water
¾ tsp salt
1 brown onion
2 carrots
¼ cabbage
4 eggs
pinch of salt
500g pork mince
1 clove garlic, minced (optional)
1 tbsp soy sauce
250g frozen peas
⅓ cup honey soy dressing (see page 155)

1. Combine rice, water and first measure of salt in a medium-sized lidded pot and bring to the boil. As soon as it boils, cover with a lid and reduce to lowest heat to cook for 12 minutes. Turn off heat and leave to steam, still covered, for a further 8 minutes. Do not lift lid during cooking or steaming. Spread cooked rice on a tray to cool slightly.
2. While rice is cooking, prepare vegetables. Finely dice onion; grate carrots; thinly slice cabbage until you have 3–4 cups worth. Set all aside.
3. Whisk eggs with second measure of salt in a medium-sized bowl.
4. When rice is at the steaming stage, prepare the rest of the meal. Heat a little oil in a large frying pan on a medium-high heat. Pour eggs into pan and allow to set for about 2 minutes until base is lightly golden. When eggs are cooked, transfer to a board or plate, thinly slice then set aside.
5. Return pan to same heat, add a little oil and cook onion for 1–2 minutes, until softened. Add mince, garlic (if using) and soy sauce and cook, breaking up mince with a wooden spoon, for 4–5 minutes, until cooked through. Remove from pan and set aside in a large bowl.
6. Return pan to same heat, add a little more oil and stir-fry carrots, cabbage and peas for 2–3 minutes. Remove from pan and add to bowl with mince.
7. Reduce heat to low-medium. Add cooked rice and honey soy dressing to pan and stir-fry for 1 minute. Return mince and veggies to pan and toss to combine. Alternatively, add stir-fried rice to bowl with cooked mince and veggies and stir to combine. Season to taste with extra soy sauce, if desired.

TO SERVE, divide pork fried rice among bowls and top with sliced egg.

ENERGY 2763KJ (660kcal)
CARBS 80.6g
PROTEIN 43.2g
FAT 17.2g

SERVES 4
PREP TIME 15 minutes
COOK TIME 20 minutes
READY IN 30 minutes

Steamy Fish Parcels

A family-friendly take on fish en papillote (fish in paper), these tasty Thai-inspired parcels are a great way to get the kids involved in cooking.

- 600g boneless, skinless, white fish fillets
- 3 tbsp soy sauce
- 1 tbsp finely grated ginger
- 1 clove garlic, minced
- 1 tbsp sweet chilli sauce (preferably mild)
- ½ tsp runny honey
- zest of 1 lemon
- 2–3 handfuls baby spinach leaves
- ½ capsicum, core and seeds removed, finely diced
- ½ red onion, thinly sliced

To serve

- 400g dried egg noodles (or your favourite fresh or dried Asian noodles)
- 1 head broccoli
- 1 lemon, cut into wedges

PREHEAT oven to 200°C. Set aside an oven tray. Bring two medium-sized pots of salted water to the boil. Cut 4 large squares of baking paper and foil (measuring about 30cm x 30cm).

1. Lay foil squares on a flat surface and place a piece of baking paper on top of each. Pat fish dry with paper towels and cut any larger fillets in half.
2. Place some fish in the centre of each square, and season with salt and freshly ground black pepper. In a small bowl, mix together soy sauce, ginger, garlic, sweet chilli sauce, honey and lemon zest, and spoon over fish. Top with spinach, capsicum and onion.
3. Wrap paper/foil up into parcels by pulling two sides up and rolling together towards fish. Twist each end of the parcel tightly, ensuring sauce does not leak out. Place onto oven tray and bake for 15–18 minutes (depending on thickness), until fish is just cooked through and vegetables are still crunchy.
4. While fish is baking, add noodles to first pot of boiling water and cook for 9–10 minutes (or according to packet instructions) until just tender. Drain and toss with a little oil to prevent sticking. Cover to keep warm.
5. While noodles are cooking, cut broccoli into small florets and dice stem into 1cm pieces. Add broccoli to second pot of boiling water and cook for 3–4 minutes, until bright green and tender, then drain. Season with salt and freshly ground black pepper.

TO SERVE, open parcels (being careful of steam) and place noodles and broccoli to one side of the fish. Place a parcel on each plate and serve with a lemon wedge for squeezing.

COOK'S HINT

Only open one parcel to check if your fish is cooked, in case you need to return them to the oven. If preferred, place noodles and broccoli onto plates and top with fish parcel contents.

ENERGY 1905KJ (455kcal)
CARBS 52.7g
PROTEIN 45.4g
FAT 6.7g

SERVES 6
PREP TIME 15 minutes
COOK TIME 25 minutes
READY IN 35 minutes

Rice

2 cups basmati rice
3 cups water
pinch of salt

Butter chicken

600g boneless, skinless chicken breasts
1 tbsp butter chicken spice mix (see below)
pinch of chilli flakes (optional)
1½ tbsp finely grated ginger
1 tsp salt
2½ tbsp butter
½ brown onion, thinly sliced
1 clove garlic, minced
1 cup cream
½ cup milk
½ cup tomato paste
¼ tsp vinegar (e.g. white wine, red wine, cider)
1 tsp sweet chilli sauce (preferably mild)

Butter chicken spice mix

Mix together 1½ tsp turmeric, 1½ tsp ground cinnamon and a small pinch chilli powder (to your taste)

To serve

1 head broccoli, cut into small florets
2 carrots, peeled, cut in half lengthways, thinly sliced
1-2 tbsp roughly chopped coriander (optional)

ENERGY 2604KJ (622kcal)
CARBS 56.8g
PROTEIN 31.7g
FAT 29.1g

Ultimate Butter Chicken

This curry is our tried-and-tested family favourite, creamy and packed with flavour — the kids will be licking their plates.

BRING a medium-sized pot of salted water to the boil.

1. Combine all rice ingredients in a medium-sized lidded pot and bring to the boil. As soon as it boils, cover with a tight-fitting lid and reduce to lowest heat to cook for 12 minutes. Turn off heat and leave to steam, still covered, for a further 8 minutes. Do not lift lid during cooking or steaming. When rice has finished steaming, fluff up grains with a fork.
2. While rice is cooking, pat chicken dry with paper towels, dice into 2cm pieces and place in a bowl with butter chicken spice mix, chilli flakes (if using), ginger and salt and mix to combine. Season with freshly ground black pepper.
3. Heat butter in a large frying pan on a medium heat. Cook onion for 4–5 minutes, until soft but not coloured. Add garlic and cook for a further 2 minutes. Add chicken and cook for 3–5 minutes, turning, until golden brown and nearly cooked through.
4. Add cream, milk, tomato paste, vinegar and sweet chilli sauce and stir to combine. Bring to a simmer, then reduce heat to low-medium and simmer for about 5 minutes, until chicken is cooked through and the sauce has thickened slightly. If the sauce thickens too much, stir through a little water.
5. While butter chicken sauce is cooking, add broccoli and carrots to pot of boiling water. Cook for 3–4 minutes, until tender. Drain well and toss with a little olive oil. Season with salt and freshly ground black pepper.

TO SERVE, spoon rice onto plates and top with butter chicken. Serve veggies on the side. Garnish your meal with fresh coriander, if desired.

DID YOU KNOW?

'Curry' comes from *kari*, the Tamil word for 'spiced sauce'. The earliest traces of curry-style cooking date back more than 4000 years.

KID
APPROVED

SERVES 4
PREP TIME 25 minutes
COOK TIME 30 minutes
READY IN 40 minutes

Chicken Skewers with Roast Potato Salad

You will need 10–12 bamboo skewers for this recipe.

Roast potato salad

800g potatoes, scrubbed and diced 2cm
1 tbsp chicken and potato spice mix (see below)
250g frozen corn kernels
½ capsicum, core and seeds removed
½ red onion
2–3 handfuls baby spinach leaves

Chicken skewers

10–12 bamboo skewers
1½ tbsp chicken and potato spice mix (see below)
2 tbsp soy sauce
¼ tsp pepper
1 tbsp olive oil
¼ tsp salt
½ tsp brown or white sugar
2 cloves garlic, minced (optional)
600g boneless, skinless chicken breasts

Chicken and potato spice mix

Mix together 1 tbsp dried oregano, 1 tbsp garlic powder, 1 tbsp ground cumin and 1½ tsp dried parsley

½ cup sour cream, to serve

ENERGY 2053KJ (491kcal)
CARBS 38.9g
PROTEIN 39.4g
FAT 18.9g

PREHEAT oven to 220°C. Bring a full kettle to the boil. Line two oven trays (1 regular, 1 lipped) with baking paper. Preheat barbecue hot plate to medium-high (if using to cook chicken). Bring a small pot of salted water to the boil. Soak bamboo skewers in water for at least 10 minutes.

1. Toss potatoes on non-lipped tray with first measure of chicken and potato spice mix and a little oil. Season with salt and freshly ground black pepper and cook for 25–30 minutes, until golden and cooked through. Turn once during cooking.
2. While potatoes are cooking, mix second measure of chicken and potato spice mix, soy sauce, pepper, olive oil, salt, sugar and garlic (if using) together in a bowl. Pat chicken dry with paper towels and cut into long, thin 1cm-wide strips. Add to marinade, mix to combine and set aside while you prepare the rest of the meal.
3. Add corn to pot of boiling water and cook for 2–3 minutes. Drain and place in a large bowl.
4. While corn cooks, prepare remaining veggies. Dice capsicum 1cm; finely dice onion; roughly chop baby spinach leaves. Add all to bowl with drained corn and set aside.
5. Thread chicken strips onto skewers, 2–3 pieces per skewer depending on the length of each chicken piece, making about 10 skewers in total. Place on lipped tray and bake for 10–12 minutes, until golden and cooked through. Alternatively, cook on barbecue grill or hot plate for 10–12 minutes, turning regularly so all sides cook evenly.
6. When potatoes are cooked, add to bowl with other salad ingredients. Toss well and season to taste with freshly ground black pepper.

TO SERVE, divide roast potato salad among plates and top with chicken skewers. Serve sour cream on the side for dipping.

SERVES 5
PREP TIME 15 minutes
COOK TIME 25 minutes
READY IN 40 minutes

Thai Pork Patties with Coconut Rice

Coconut rice is very popular with kids. The coconut gives it a slight sweetness, which they love!

Coconut rice

2 cups jasmine rice
165ml can coconut cream
2⅓ cups water

Thai pork patties

600g pork mince
1 egg
1 clove garlic, minced
1 tbsp finely grated ginger
1 spring onion, cut in half lengthways, thinly sliced
1 tbsp Thai spice mix (see below)
2 tbsp soy sauce
½ tsp salt
zest of 1 lemon
1 tbsp sweet chilli sauce (preferably mild)

Thai salad

2 stalks celery
1 capsicum
½ telegraph cucumber
1 carrot
3 tbsp Thai dressing (see page 155)

Thai spice mix

Mix together 1 tsp garlic powder, ½ tsp coriander flakes, ½ tsp ground cumin, ½ tsp ground ginger, ¼ tsp black pepper and ¼ tsp dried mint

1 lemon, cut into wedges, to serve

ENERGY 2473KJ (591kcal)
CARBS 71.2g
PROTEIN 32.3g
FAT 619.7g

PREHEAT barbecue hot plate to high (if using to cook pork patties).

1. Combine rice, coconut cream, water and a good pinch of salt in a medium-sized lidded pot and bring to the boil. As soon as it boils, stir, cover with a tight-fitting lid and reduce to lowest heat to cook for 15 minutes. Turn off heat and leave to steam, still covered, for a further 10 minutes. Do not lift lid during cooking or steaming. When rice has finished steaming, fluff up grains with a fork.
2. While rice cooks, prepare Thai pork patties. Using clean hands, mix all Thai pork patty ingredients in a large bowl until well combined. Use a ¼ cup measure to scoop out mixture and roll into balls. Flatten slightly with a fork until patties are about 1.5cm thick.
3. Heat a little oil in a large frying pan on a medium-high heat. Cook patties, in batches, for 2–3 minutes each side, until cooked through and browned. Wipe out pan between batches and add more oil if needed. Set aside, covered, to keep warm as you cook the remaining patties. Alternatively, cook on barbecue hot plate following the same method.
4. While patties cook, prepare Thai salad. Thinly slice celery on an angle; remove core and seeds from capsicum and thinly slice; cut cucumber into thin matchsticks; grate carrot. Place all in a medium-sized bowl with Thai dressing and mix to combine. Season to taste with salt and freshly ground black pepper.

TO SERVE, divide coconut rice among plates and top with Thai pork patties and Thai salad. Drizzle patties with extra sweet chilli sauce (if desired), and serve a lemon wedge on the side for squeezing.

COOK'S HINT

Store any remaining Thai dressing in an airtight container in the fridge for a later date. Garnish your patties with fresh coriander or parsley if you have some on hand.

CATCH OF THE DAY

SERVES 5
PREP TIME 15 minutes
COOK TIME 20 minutes
READY IN 30 minutes

Coconut Fish Curry

This curry is so tasty, it will have you coming back for more!

Rice

2 cups jasmine rice
3 cups water
pinch of salt

Coconut fish curry

1 brown onion, thinly sliced
1 carrot, cut in half lengthways, thinly sliced
2 tbsp finely grated ginger
1 tbsp curry spice mix (see below)
1 cup water
400ml can coconut cream
1 tbsp soy sauce
1 tsp sugar
600g boneless, skinless, white fish fillets
2–3 handfuls baby spinach leaves
juice of ½ lemon

Curry spice mix

Mix together 1 tsp powdered vegetable stock, 1 tsp ground turmeric and 1 tsp curry powder

1. Combine all rice ingredients in a medium-sized lidded pot and bring to the boil. As soon as it boils, cover with a tight-fitting lid and reduce to lowest heat to cook for 12 minutes. Turn off heat and leave to steam, still covered, for a further 8 minutes. Do not lift lid during cooking or steaming. When rice has finished steaming, fluff up grains with a fork.
2. Heat a little oil in a large frying pan (or medium-sized pot) on a medium heat. Cook onion for 2–3 minutes, until softened. Add carrot, ginger and curry spice mix and cook for a further 1–2 minutes, until fragrant.
3. Add water, coconut cream, soy sauce and sugar. Bring to a simmer and cook for 4–5 minutes, until vegetables are starting to soften.
4. Pat fish dry with paper towels and season with salt and freshly ground black pepper. Place whole fish fillets into coconut sauce, ensuring fish is submerged. Bring to a simmer and cook gently for about 6 minutes, until fish is just cooked through.
5. Gently stir through spinach and lemon juice and season to taste with salt and freshly ground black pepper.

TO SERVE, spoon rice onto each plate or bowl and top with coconut fish curry.

ENERGY 2577KJ (616kcal)
CARBS 70.6g
PROTEIN 26.8g
FAT 25.4g

COOK'S HINT

A firm-fleshed fish will work best in this curry — try trevally, kahawai or monkfish the next time you make it.

KIWI FAVS

THESE DISHES will *never* go out of style, especially when you jazz them up with fresh, modern flavours! Hearty and delicious, they're the kind of meals that bring back memories of good times with the people you love. We couldn't imagine putting together a cookbook without them! After all, who doesn't love sausage rolls, meatloaf or barbecued chicken? And for those nights when you want a healthy takeaway substitute, you can't go past homemade fish 'n' chips!

SERVES 6
PREP TIME 15 minutes
COOK TIME 30 minutes
READY IN 40 minutes

Chicken 'n' Kumara Pie

Comfort food at its finest, this deliciously creamy pie has a nice hint of sweetness from the kumara, which we reckon kids will love.

Kumara top

800g orange kumara, peeled and diced 2–3cm
1 tbsp butter
1 tsp salt
1 cup grated cheese

Chicken pie filling

600g boneless, skinless chicken thighs
1 brown onion
½ bunch silverbeet
3 tbsp butter
¼ cup flour
1 cup milk
½ cup chicken stock
1 cup frozen corn kernels
1 tsp salt

To serve

1 head broccoli, cut into small florets
1 carrot, halved lengthways, then thinly sliced
1 tbsp butter (optional)

PREHEAT oven grill to 200°C/high. Bring a large pot of salted water to the boil. Set aside a large casserole dish (measuring about 30cm x 22cm).

1. Cook kumara in pot of boiling water for 15–20 minutes, until soft. Drain, return to pot and mash with butter and salt until smooth. Cover and set aside.
2. Pat chicken dry with paper towels, dice 3cm and season with salt and freshly ground black pepper. Finely dice onion and finely chop silverbeet leaves and stalks until you have about 3 cups worth.
3. Heat a little oil in a large frying pan on a high heat. Cook chicken and onion for 4–5 minutes, until onion has softened. Reduce heat to medium, add butter and cook for 1 minute. Add flour and cook for 1 minute, stirring. Gradually add milk and stock, stirring to avoid any lumps.
4. Bring to a simmer and cook for 5–7 minutes, until thickened. Add silverbeet, corn and salt. Cook a further 1–2 minutes, until silverbeet has wilted. Season to taste with freshly ground black pepper. Add pie filling to oven dish, top with kumara mash and spread out evenly. Sprinkle over cheese. Grill (on upper oven rack) for about 4 minutes or until cheese is golden.
5. Bring 1 cup of salted water to the boil in a medium-sized pot. Add broccoli and carrot. Cover and steam until bright and tender, about 2–3 minutes. Drain and toss with butter (if using) and season with salt and freshly ground black pepper.

TO SERVE, divide chicken 'n' kumara pie among plates and serve vegetables on the side.

ENERGY 2461KJ (588kcal)
CARBS 41.7g
PROTEIN 30.1g
FAT 32.4g

FUN FACT

Kumara, also known as sweet potato in other parts of the world, was brought to New Zealand by Māori from Polynesia.

KID
APPROVED

SERVES 4
PREP TIME 25 minutes
COOK TIME 30 minutes
READY IN 45 minutes

BBQ Chicken Meatballs with Potato Salad

The delicious potato salad is also great to accompany other proteins including chicken skewers, nibbles or drumsticks.

Potato salad

800g potatoes, scrubbed and diced 3cm
½ cup drained gherkins
3 stalks celery
2 spring onions
2 tbsp mayo
¼ cup natural yoghurt
2 tbsp mustard (e.g. wholegrain, Dijon)
2 tbsp vinegar (e.g. white wine, red wine, cider)
½ tsp salt
2–3 handfuls baby spinach leaves

Chicken meatballs

250g frozen corn kernels, defrosted
½ brown onion, finely diced
600g chicken mince
½ tsp salt
1 egg
1 tsp soy sauce
1 cup fine breadcrumbs

Barbecue sauce

100g BBQ sauce
2 tbsp water

PREHEAT oven to 220°C. Bring a medium-sized pot of salted water to the boil. Preheat a large oven-proof dish (measuring about 30cm x 20cm).

1. Cook potatoes in pot of boiling water for 12–15 minutes, until tender. Drain and run under a cold tap to cool slightly. Drain well.
2. While potatoes are cooking, prepare the rest of the meal. Roughly chop gherkins and thinly slice celery and spring onions. In a large bowl, whisk mayo, yoghurt, mustard, vinegar and salt together. Add gherkins, celery, spring onion and spinach to bowl with dressing. Set aside.
3. Add corn to a large bowl with all remaining chicken meatball ingredients and season with freshly ground black pepper. Use clean hands to mix until well combined.
4. Using a ¼ cup measure, scoop out mixture and shape into golf-ball-sized balls. Set aside on a plate or tray. In a small bowl, combine BBQ sauce and water.
5. Remove preheated dish from oven and put a little oil on the base. Put meatballs into dish and bake for 6 minutes. Remove from oven and evenly spoon over BBQ sauce mixture. Gently turn meatballs to coat in sauce. Return to oven to cook for a further 12–15 minutes, until cooked through.
6. Toss cooked potatoes in bowl with dressing and veggies until combined. Season to taste with salt and freshly ground black pepper.

TO SERVE, divide potato salad and BBQ chicken meatballs between plates.

ENERGY 2505KJ (599kcal)
CARBS 62.5g
PROTEIN 40.4g
FAT 19.2g

TIME-SAVER

Roll meatballs in advance and store, covered, in the fridge to save time on the night.

FRIDAY
SPECIAL

SERVES 4
PREP TIME 20 minutes
COOK TIME 30 minutes
READY IN 35 minutes

Fish 'n' Chips with Greens

We hope you enjoy our healthy 'take on the takeaways' with this delicious and simple Friday special.

Chips

800g potatoes, scrubbed and cut into 2cm-thick chips

Fish

600g boneless, skinless, white fish fillets
1 cup panko breadcrumbs
zest of 1 lemon
juice of ½ lemon
2 tbsp oil or melted butter
2 tbsp mayo

Greens

2 cups water
1 head broccoli, florets and stem finely chopped
250g frozen peas, defrosted
1 tbsp butter
2–3 handfuls baby spinach leaves, roughly chopped

To serve

½ cup tartare sauce (store-bought or see page 155)
½ lemon, cut into wedges

PREHEAT oven to 220°C. Line two oven trays with baking paper.

1. Toss potatoes on first prepared tray with a little oil and season with salt and freshly ground black pepper. Bake for 25–30 minutes, until golden and cooked through. Turn once during cooking.
2. Pat fish dry with paper towels. Cut fillets into 5cm pieces, lay on second prepared tray and season with salt. In a small bowl, mix together breadcrumbs, lemon zest and juice and oil/butter.
3. Evenly spread mayo on top of fish. Spoon crumb on top and push down lightly to help adhere. When potatoes have about 10 minutes of cooking time remaining, bake fish. Bake (on rack above potatoes), for 6–8 minutes (depending on thickness), until just cooked through and crumb is golden. Take care not to let crumb burn.
4. While the fish cooks, bring water to the boil in a medium-sized lidded pot. When boiling, add broccoli and cook, covered, for 3 minutes. Add peas and cook for a further 3 minutes, until soft. Drain and roughly mash with butter. Stir through spinach and season to taste with salt and freshly ground black pepper.

TO SERVE, divide fish 'n' chips and greens among plates. Serve with a dollop of tartare sauce and a lemon wedge to squeeze over just before eating.

ENERGY 2442KJ (584kcal)
CARBS 51.0g
PROTEIN 36.9g
FAT 24.1g

FUN FACT

Fish 'n' chips — they're part of our DNA as Kiwis! We love them with tomato sauce, but in the UK it's common to splash malt vinegar on your fish 'n' chips for added seasoning. What do you think?

SERVES 5
PREP TIME 20 minutes
COOK TIME 30 minutes
READY IN 40 minutes

Smoked Paprika Chicken with Potato Salad

A taste of summer, this smoky chicken with potato salad is the perfect meal to take outside on a warm evening.

Potato salad

800g potatoes, scrubbed and diced 2–3cm
1 tsp smoked paprika
1 capsicum
½ red onion
2–3 handfuls baby spinach leaves
1 cup grated cheese
½ cup sour cream
2 tbsp mayo
1 tsp mustard (e.g. Dijon, wholegrain)

Smoked paprika chicken

600g boneless, skinless chicken thighs
zest of 1 orange
¾ tsp smoked paprika
1 tsp mustard (eg. Dijon, wholegrain)
2 tbsp tomato sauce
1 tbsp sweet chilli sauce (preferably mild)

PREHEAT oven to 220°C. Line an oven tray with baking paper. Preheat barbecue grill or hot plate to medium-high (if using to cook chicken).

1. Toss potatoes on prepared tray with smoked paprika and a little oil. Season with salt and freshly ground black pepper and bake for 25–30 minutes, until golden and cooked through. Turn once during cooking. Set aside to cool slightly.
2. While potatoes are cooking, prepare chicken. Pat chicken dry with paper towels and place in a large bowl with orange zest, smoked paprika, mustard, tomato sauce and sweet chilli sauce. Season with salt and freshly ground black pepper and mix to combine. Set aside to marinate for 10–15 minutes.
3. While potatoes are cooking and chicken is marinating, prepare the rest of the salad. Remove core and seeds from capsicum and thinly slice. Finely slice onion and roughly chop baby spinach. Place all in a large bowl with cheese. Mix sour cream, mayo and mustard together in a small bowl and set aside.
4. Heat a little oil in a large frying pan on a medium heat. Cook chicken for 4–5 minutes each side, until cooked through. Alternatively, cook on barbecue grill or hot plate using the same method. Set aside on a plate, covered in foil, to rest for 2–3 minutes, then slice.
5. Place cooled potatoes into bowl with salad ingredients and mix gently to combine. Add sour cream and mayo mix and stir to coat salad. Season to taste with salt and freshly ground black pepper.

TO SERVE, place a large spoonful of salad onto each plate and top with smoked paprika chicken.

ENERGY 2389KJ (571kcal)
CARBS 29.9g
PROTEIN 31.9g
FAT 35.9g

COOK'S HINT

This chicken is ideal for the BBQ — its smoky flavour will be enhanced with a bit of char from the grill!

SERVES 4
PREP TIME 20 minutes
COOK TIME 120 minutes
READY IN 135 minutes

Slow-Cooked Beef Stew with Leafy Mash

This is a great one to pop in the slow cooker so you can enjoy a dinner with maximum flavour and minimum stress!

Slow-cooked beef stew

1 brown onion, finely diced
2 cloves garlic, finely diced
2 stalks celery, diced 1cm
1 carrot, diced 1cm
1 tbsp dried herb mix (see below)
1 tbsp flour, seasoned with 1 tsp salt
600g stewing beef, diced 3cm (at room temperature)
¾ cup water
5 tbsp tomato paste
1 cup beef stock
400g can chopped tomatoes
1½ tbsp soy sauce
1 tbsp tomato sauce
2–3 handfuls baby spinach leaves

Dried herb mix

Mix together 1 tsp dried rosemary, 1 tsp dried oregano, ½ tsp onion powder and ½ tsp garlic powder

Leafy mash

800g potatoes, peeled
1 tbsp butter
¼ cup milk
2 tbsp wholegrain mustard
2–3 handfuls baby spinach leaves

ENERGY 2228KJ (533kcal)
CARBS 44.4g
PROTEIN 41.2g
FAT 19.6g

PREHEAT oven to 160°C. Preheat a medium-sized casserole dish (measuring about 20cm x 30cm and preferably lidded). Alternatively, turn on slow cooker.

1. Heat a little oil in a large frying pan on a medium heat. Cook onion, garlic, celery, carrot and dried herb mix for 5–6 minutes, stirring, until fragrant and vegetables are starting to soften. Transfer to preheated casserole dish (don't return to oven yet). Return pan to a medium-high heat with a little more oil. Place seasoned flour on a plate, pat beef dry and toss in flour to coat.
2. Add beef to pan and cook, stirring, for 4–5 minutes, until browned all over. Add water, tomato paste, stock and canned tomatoes and bring to a simmer. Use a wooden spoon to scrape the bottom of the pan before transferring to casserole dish with vegetables.
3. Stir, cover with a tight-fitting lid or foil and bake for about 1 hour 45 minutes, or until beef is tender. (Alternatively, cook in slow cooker for 4–4.5 hours on high, or 8–8.5 hours on low.) Remove from oven and stir through soy sauce, tomato sauce and baby spinach and season to taste with salt and freshly ground black pepper.
4. When stew has about 30 minutes of cooking time remaining, bring a large pot of salted water to the boil. Dice potatoes into 3cm pieces, add to pot and cook for about 15 minutes, until very soft. Drain, return to pot and mash with butter, milk and mustard until smooth.
5. Roughly chop baby spinach, stir through mash and season to taste with salt and freshly ground black pepper.

TO SERVE, spoon leafy mash onto plates and top with slow-cooked beef stew.

KID
APPROVE

SERVES 6
PREP TIME 15 minutes
COOK TIME 35 minutes
READY IN 50 minutes

Chicken Filo Pie

Our take on a chicken pot pie, enjoy this moreish and family-friendly recipe that's full of flavour.

- 600g boneless, skinless chicken thighs, diced 2cm
- 1 brown onion, finely diced
- 1 carrot, grated
- 3 tbsp butter
- ¼ cup flour
- 2 tbsp mustard (e.g. wholegrain, Dijon)
- 1½ tbsp herb spice mix (see below)
- 1 tsp salt
- 1 cup chicken or vegetable stock
- ½ cup water
- ½ cup sour cream
- 250g frozen peas
- 6–8 sheets filo pastry
- 2–3 tbsp melted butter or oil

Herb spice mix

Mix together 2 tsp dried parsley, 2 tsp garlic powder, 1 tsp onion powder and ½ tsp dried basil

1 head broccoli, cut into small florets and stem diced 1cm, to serve

PREHEAT oven to 200°C. Grease a large casserole dish (measuring about 20cm x 30cm) with melted butter or oil.

1. Heat a little oil in a large frying pan on a medium-high heat. Cook chicken for 2–3 minutes, until starting to brown. Add onion and carrot and cook for a further 2–3 minutes, until vegetables have softened. Reduce heat to medium, add butter and cook for 1 minute. Add flour and cook for 2 minutes, stirring constantly. Add mustard, herb spice mix and salt. Gradually add stock, then water, stirring constantly to avoid any lumps forming.
2. Reduce heat to low-medium. Add sour cream and peas and cook for a further 1–2 minutes, until heated through. Season to taste with freshly ground black pepper. Place pie filling in casserole dish.
3. Brush each filo pastry rectangle lightly with melted butter or oil. Very loosely scrunch filo up and place on top of the filling, putting the pieces side by side, until the surface of the pie is completely covered.
4. Once topped with filo, bake chicken filo pie for about 15 minutes, until filo topping is golden and crunchy. Cool for 5 minutes before serving.
5. While pie is baking, bring a medium-sized pot of salted water to the boil. Cook broccoli in pot of boiling water for 3–4 minutes, until bright green and tender. Drain, toss with a little olive oil and season with salt and freshly ground black pepper.

TO SERVE, cut chicken filo pie into 6 portions with a large spoon and divide among plates. Serve broccoli on the side.

ENERGY 2083KJ (498kcal)
CARBS 25.2g
PROTEIN 26.3g
FAT 31.9g

SERVES 6
PREP TIME 20 minutes
COOK TIME 30 minutes
READY IN 50 minutes

Scrummy Sausage Rolls

These sausage rolls are delicious for dinner with a fresh side salad or to enjoy as leftovers for lunch.

Sausage rolls

1 brown onion, finely diced
1 apple, grated
½ carrot, grated
500g good-quality sausages, filling removed from casing
1 cup panko breadcrumbs
1 egg
¾ tsp salt
3 sheets frozen puff pastry squares, defrosted
2 tbsp milk

Salad

½ iceberg lettuce
½ carrot
1 tomato
2 corn cobs, husk and silk removed
1 tbsp mayo
1 tsp vinegar (e.g. red wine, white wine, cider)

tomato sauce, to serve (optional)

PREHEAT oven to 200°C. Line an oven tray with baking paper. Bring a small pot of salted water to the boil.

1. Heat a little oil in a large frying pan on a medium heat and cook onion, apple and carrot for 3–4 minutes, until soft. While vegetables are cooking, combine sausage filling, breadcrumbs, egg and salt in a bowl. Add cooked vegetables to bowl and use a wooden spoon to combine well.
2. Place pastry squares on a flat surface, and cut in half with a sharp knife so you have 2 rectangles with short sides facing you (6 in total).
3. Divide sausage mixture into 6 even portions and mould a portion into a log shape on the bottom third of each pastry piece. Roll pastry and sausage mixture away from you to enclose tightly, with about 2cm overlap of pastry for the seam. Trim off any excess pastry and reserve. Place roll on prepared tray, seam-side down.
4. Brush sausage rolls with milk and bake for 25–30 minutes, until pastry is puffed and golden. Leave to cool on tray for at least 5 minutes before serving.
5. While sausage rolls are cooking, prepare the salad. Thinly slice lettuce; grate carrot; dice tomato into 1cm pieces. Cut corn off cobs and place into pot of boiling water for 3–4 minutes, refresh with cold water and drain well. Place all in a medium-sized bowl with mayo and vinegar. Season to taste with salt and freshly ground black pepper and toss to combine.

TO SERVE, divide sausage rolls between plates and top with tomato sauce (if using). Serve salad on the side.

WHY NOT TRY?

To use up your leftover pastry, spread with Vegemite or Marmite and sprinkle with cheese, roll up tightly and slice into 2–3 pieces. Bake for 10–15 minutes at 180°C, until golden.

ENERGY 2357KJ (564 kcal)
CARBS 50.8g
PROTEIN 25.9g
FAT 27.9g

UNDER
30 MINS

SERVES 5
PREP TIME 35 minutes
COOK TIME 15 minutes
READY IN 25 minutes

Sticky Apricot Chicken with Rice Salad

Apricot chicken — not only delicious but a tasty use for that jar of apricot jam sitting in the back of your cupboard.

Rice salad

1½ cups jasmine rice
2¼ cups water
pinch of salt
1 carrot
1 courgette
1 capsicum
1–2 handfuls baby spinach leaves
1–2 tbsp apricot jam
1 tsp wholegrain mustard
3 tbsp mayo
1½ tbsp lemon juice
1 tsp salt

Sticky apricot chicken

600g boneless, skinless chicken thighs
1 tbsp water
¼ cup apricot jam
½ tsp wholegrain mustard

chopped coriander, to serve (optional)

PREHEAT oven to 220°C. Set aside a large baking dish or oven tray (with a lip). Preheat barbecue hot plate to medium-high (if using to cook chicken).

1. Combine rice, water and salt in a medium-sized lidded pot and bring to the boil. As soon as it boils, cover with a tight-fitting lid and reduce to lowest heat to cook for 12 minutes. Turn off heat and leave to steam, still covered, for a further 8 minutes. Do not lift lid during cooking or steaming. Spread cooked rice on a tray and place in fridge for 10 minutes to cool.
2. While rice is cooking, pat chicken dry with paper towels. Place chicken in baking dish or oven tray and season with salt and freshly ground black pepper.
3. Mix water, apricot jam and mustard together in a small bowl. Spread mixture over chicken and roast for about 20 minutes, or until cooked through. Remove from oven and set aside to rest, covered in foil, for about 5 minutes before slicing thickly. Alternatively, cook sticky apricot chicken on barbecue hot plate for 4–6 minutes each side (depending on thickness), or until cooked through. Keep a close eye on chicken to ensure it doesn't burn.
4. While chicken is cooking, prepare the vegetables and dressing for the rice salad. Peel carrot; grate carrot and courgette; remove core and seeds from capsicum and finely dice; thinly slice spinach. Place all in a large bowl.
5. Mix together apricot jam, mustard, mayo, lemon juice and salt in a small bowl. Add dressing to bowl with vegetables along with cooked rice and mix to combine. Season with freshly ground black pepper.

TO SERVE, spoon rice salad onto plates and top with sticky apricot chicken. Sprinkle with chopped coriander, if desired.

ENERGY 2412KJ (576kcal)
CARBS 63.7g
PROTEIN 25.5g
FAT 24.4g

KID
APPROVED

SERVES 4
PREP TIME 15 minutes
COOK TIME 30 minutes
READY IN 35 minutes

Fish 'n' Creamy Leeks with Roasties

Fish is a great protein to eat at least once a week. We're making it easy for you with this scrumptious option.

Roasties

800g potatoes, scrubbed and diced 2–3cm

Fish 'n' creamy leeks

2 spring onions, white and pale green part only (reserve dark green part to serve)
1 leek, white and pale green part only
600g boneless, skinless, white fish fillets
3 tbsp flour, seasoned with ½ tsp salt
zest of 1 lemon
2 tbsp butter
1 clove garlic, finely chopped
¾ cup chicken stock
1 tsp mustard (e.g. wholegrain, Dijon)
¼ tsp salt
100ml cream

To serve

1 head broccoli
1 lemon, cut into wedges
2 spring onions, dark green part only, thinly sliced

PREHEAT oven to 220°C. Line an oven tray with baking paper.

1. Toss potatoes with a little oil on prepared tray. Season with salt and freshly ground black pepper and bake for 25–30 minutes, until golden and cooked through. Turn once during cooking.
2. While potatoes are cooking, prepare the rest of the meal. Thinly slice spring onions and cut leek in half lengthways and thinly slice. Set aside.
3. Pat fish dry with paper towels and cut any larger fillets into 2–3 pieces. Place seasoned flour and lemon zest on a large plate and season with freshly ground black pepper. Dust fish in flour mixture. Heat a little oil in a large frying pan on a medium heat. Cook fish for 2–3 minutes each side, until golden and nearly cooked through. Set aside, covered with foil.
4. Heat butter in same pan on a medium heat and cook spring onion, leek and garlic for 5–6 minutes, stirring, until softened. Add stock, mustard and salt, bring to a simmer and cook for 2 minutes. Stir through cream and cook for a further 2 minutes, until thickened slightly. Season to taste with freshly ground black pepper.
5. Add cooked fish to pan with creamy leeks on medium heat. Gently turn fish a few times to coat in sauce and cook for a further 1–2 minutes, until fish is cooked through.
6. While leeks and fish are cooking, bring a medium-sized pot of salted water to the boil and cut broccoli into florets. Cook broccoli in pot of boiling water for 2–3 minutes, until bright green and tender. Drain.

TO SERVE, divide roasties and fish 'n' creamy leeks between plates. Serve with a wedge of lemon to squeeze over fish just before eating. Garnish with green part of spring onion and serve broccoli on the side.

ENERGY 1993KJ (476kcal)
CARBS 40.5g
PROTEIN 32.5g
FAT 19.1g

SERVES 4
PREP TIME 20 minutes
COOK TIME 20 minutes
READY IN 35 minutes

Zingy BBQ Chicken with Smashed Potato 'n' Peas

This chicken will have you licking your lips! Consider making extra for lunch as this will be a crowd-pleaser.

Zingy BBQ chicken

600g boneless, skinless chicken thighs
3 tbsp tomato sauce
2 tbsp sweet chilli sauce (preferably mild)
1 tbsp soy sauce
1 tbsp olive oil
1 tbsp vinegar (e.g. white wine, red wine)
½ tsp salt
1 tsp Cajun spice mix (see below)

Cajun spice mix

Mix together ¼ tsp garlic powder, ¼ tsp paprika, ¼ tsp dried oregano, ¼ tsp dried thyme, ⅛ tsp onion powder, and a very small pinch black pepper and cayenne pepper

Smashed potato 'n' peas

800g potatoes, scrubbed and diced 1-2cm
250g frozen peas
1-2 tbsp butter
2 tbsp milk
1-2 tbsp mayo (optional)

Salad

1 capsicum
2 tomatoes
½ telegraph cucumber
2-3 handfuls baby spinach leaves
1 tbsp olive oil
1½ tbsp vinegar (e.g. white wine, red wine)

ENERGY 2686KJ (642kcal)
CARBS 45.3g
PROTEIN 36.4g
FAT 33.8g

BRING a large lidded pot of salted water to the boil. Preheat barbecue grill or hot plate to medium-high (if using to cook chicken).

1. Pat chicken dry with paper towels and place in a large bowl with all remaining zingy BBQ chicken ingredients. Mix to combine and set aside to marinate for 5–10 minutes.
2. Cook potatoes in pot of boiling water, covered, for 13–15 minutes, until soft. Add peas for last 3 minutes of cooking time. Drain and return to pot with butter, milk and mayo (if using). Lightly crush with a fork and season to taste with salt and freshly ground black pepper. Set aside and keep warm with lid on.
3. Heat a little oil in a large frying pan on a medium heat. Cook chicken, in two batches, for 4–5 minutes each side, until cooked through. Turn down heat if marinade starts to burn. Alternatively, cook on barbecue grill or hot plate using the same method. Set aside on a plate, covered in foil, to rest for 2–3 minutes.
4. While chicken and potatoes are cooking, prepare salad. Remove core and seeds from capsicum; dice capsicum, tomatoes and cucumber. Place all in a large bowl with spinach, oil and vinegar and toss to combine. Season to taste with salt and freshly ground black pepper.

TO SERVE, place a large spoonful of smashed potato 'n' peas on each plate. Slice zingy BBQ chicken into thick pieces and place on top. Serve salad on the side.

TIP

Leave out the cayenne and black pepper from the spice mix to suit your little ones.

MAKE AHEAD

SERVES 5
PREP TIME 15 minutes
COOK TIME 40 minutes
READY IN 45 minutes

Meatloaf 'n' Mash

You can't get more classic than meatloaf 'n' mash! This version is sure to be a favourite in your household — and the leftovers make the best sammies for lunch, too.

Meatloaf

1 brown onion, finely diced
1 carrot, grated
1 parsnip, peeled and grated
300g beef mince
300g pork mince
1 egg
½ cup panko breadcrumbs
1 tbsp soy sauce
½ tsp salt
¼ cup tomato sauce
½ cup grated cheese

Mash

800g potatoes
2 tbsp butter
¼ cup milk

1 head broccoli, cut into small florets and stem diced 1cm, to serve

PREHEAT oven to 200°C. Grease a large baking dish (measuring about 22cm x 28cm) with oil or butter. Bring a large pot of salted water to the boil.

1. Heat a little oil in a large frying pan on a medium heat. Cook onion, carrot and parsnip for about 4 minutes, until tender. Set aside to cool.
2. In a large bowl, combine beef and pork mince, egg, breadcrumbs, soy sauce, salt and half the tomato sauce. Season with freshly ground black pepper, add cooked vegetables and mix well. Place mixture into prepared dish and use clean hands to press in. Evenly spread remaining tomato sauce on top and finish with cheese. Bake for 25–30 minutes, until cooked through. Turn oven setting to grill and grill for 2–3 minutes, until top is golden.
3. While meatloaf is cooking, peel or scrub potatoes and dice into 3cm pieces. Cook in pot of boiling water for about 15 minutes, until very soft. Drain and mash with butter and milk until smooth. Season to taste with salt.
4. Wipe out pan used for veggies and heat a little oil on a medium heat. Stir-fry broccoli for about 2 minutes, until bright green. Add about 2 tablespoons water and stir-fry for a further 1–2 minutes, until cooked to your liking. Remove from heat and season to taste with salt and freshly ground black pepper.
5. Remove meatloaf from oven and allow to cool for 5 minutes. Cut into squares.

TO SERVE, divide meatloaf, mash and broccoli among plates.

ENERGY 2487KJ (594kcal)
CARBS 47.3g
PROTEIN 37.2g
FAT 27.4g

SERVES 4
PREP TIME 15 minutes
COOK TIME 30 minutes
READY IN 40 minutes

Lemon Chicken Thighs with Spiced Potatoes

Lemon pepper is a great spice to have on hand, it works nicely with a variety of proteins or as a light seasoning for chips.

Spiced potatoes

- 800g potatoes, scrubbed and diced 2cm
- 2 tbsp chicken spice mix (see below)
- ½ tsp salt

Lemon chicken thighs

- 600g chicken thighs
- 1 tbsp chicken spice mix (see below)
- ½ tsp salt
- juice of ½ lemon
- 2 tbsp oil

Chicken spice mix

Mix together 1 tbsp lemon pepper, 1 tbsp ground turmeric and 1 tbsp dried oregano

Salad

- 1 tomato
- ½ telegraph cucumber
- ½ iceberg lettuce
- ½ tbsp olive oil
- juice of ½ lemon

PREHEAT oven to 220°C. Line an oven tray with baking paper. Preheat barbecue hot plate to medium-high (if using to cook chicken).

1. Toss potatoes, chicken spice mix and salt on prepared tray with a little oil. Roast for 25–30 minutes, until cooked through and golden. Turn once during cooking.
2. While potatoes are cooking, pat chicken dry with paper towels. Heat a little oil in a large frying pan on a medium-high heat. Combine all remaining lemon chicken thigh ingredients in a large bowl, add chicken, and mix to coat. Season with freshly ground black pepper.
3. Cook chicken in frying pan for 4–5 minutes each side, until golden and cooked through. Alternatively, cook on barbecue hot plate using the same method.
4. While chicken is cooking, prepare the salad. Dice tomato and cucumber into 2cm pieces and roughly chop lettuce. Place in a large bowl with oil and lemon juice. Season with salt and freshly ground black pepper and mix well.

TO SERVE, divide lemon chicken thighs, spiced potatoes and salad among plates.

ENERGY 2107KJ (504kcal)
CARBS 34.0g
PROTEIN 31.5g
FAT 26.1g

COOK'S HINT

To get your potatoes nice and crispy, turn your oven setting to grill for the last 5 minutes of cook time.

WASTE NOT, WANT NOT

WHEN IT COMES to making your food budget stretch that little bit further, it pays to have some creative ideas to use up leftovers. Coming up with new ways to use leftover ingredients is an impressive skill, so we thought we'd give you the head start on a few of our favourite tricks. This section is all about tying together those unused ingredients into easy-does-it tasty treats. Leftover pastry? Bacon and egg pie for lunch! Leftover veggies? No-fuss frittata! These are recipes we swear by when it comes to using your leftovers. Waste not, want not? Absolutely!

SERVES 5
PREP TIME 25 minutes
COOK TIME 45 minutes
READY IN 55 minutes

Chicken 'n' Bacon Soup

We think soups are so underrated! They can be filling and delicious, especially when you add bacon.

Chicken 'n' bacon soup

1 tbsp butter
1 tbsp oil
1 brown onion, finely diced
1½ cloves garlic, minced
1 carrot, diced 1cm
2–3 stalks celery, diced 1cm
1 tbsp dried Italian herbs (see page 19)
½ tsp salt
200g shoulder bacon
400g boneless, skinless chicken thighs, diced 1–2cm
400g orange kumara, scrubbed and diced 1cm
2 x 400g cans chopped tomatoes
3 cups chicken or vegetable stock
1 cup boiling water
400g can cannellini beans

Garlic pita breads

2 tbsp butter, softened
½ clove garlic, minced
6 pita breads

2 tbsp parsley, roughly chopped, to serve (optional)

BRING a half-full kettle to the boil. Line an oven tray with baking paper.

1. Heat butter and oil in a large pot on a medium heat. Cook onion, garlic, carrot, celery, dried Italian herbs and salt for 3–4 minutes, until vegetables have softened. While onion cooks, remove rind from bacon (discard) and dice into 1cm pieces. Add bacon to pot and cook for a further 2–3 minutes, until starting to brown.
2. Add diced chicken to pot and cook for about 3 minutes, until starting to brown. Add kumara, canned tomatoes, stock and boiling water and bring to the boil. Reduce heat to low-medium and simmer for about 25 minutes, or until vegetables are cooked. Stir occasionally.
3. While soup simmers, preheat oven to 200°C. Drain and rinse cannellini beans. When vegetables are cooked, add cannellini beans to soup and cook for about 2 minutes, until beans are heated through. Use a potato masher to mash vegetables slightly and mix to combine. Season to taste with salt and freshly ground black pepper.
4. While soup is cooking, mix butter and garlic together in a small bowl and season with freshly ground black pepper. Spread garlic butter evenly on one side of each pita. Place pita breads on prepared tray and bake for 5–6 minutes, or until they are golden and butter is melted. Alternatively toast them without butter in the toaster. Cut pita breads into quarters.

TO SERVE, ladle chicken 'n' bacon soup into bowls, top with parsley (if using) and serve garlic pita breads on the side.

ENERGY 2448KJ (586kcal)
CARBS 60.1g
PROTEIN 31.6g
FAT 23.3g

WHY NOT TRY?

Add a pinch of chilli flakes for adults, or those who like a bit of spice!

SERVES 5
PREP TIME 15 minutes
COOK TIME 30 minutes
READY IN 40 minutes

Chicken Chowder

There's nothing like a rich chicken chowder to warm you up in winter. This one is super easy — you'll wonder how delicious can be so quick!

- 1 brown onion, finely diced
- 2 cloves garlic, minced
- 1 carrot, finely diced
- 4 stalks celery, thinly sliced
- 1 tbsp chowder herbs (see below)
- 400g potatoes, peeled and grated
- 600g boneless, skinless, chicken thighs
- 1 tsp salt
- 3 cups stock (e.g. chicken, vegetable)
- 2 cups hot water
- 250g frozen corn kernels
- ⅓ cup cream

Chowder herbs

Mix together 1 tsp dried oregano, 1 tsp smoked paprika, 1 tsp ground cumin, 1 tsp garlic powder and ¼ tsp dried sage

6 dinner rolls, to serve
butter, to serve (optional)

PREHEAT oven to 200°C to heat dinner rolls. Bring a full kettle to the boil.

1. Heat a little oil in a large pot on a medium heat. Cook onion, garlic, carrot, celery and chowder herbs for about 5 minutes, stirring regularly, until vegetables start to soften.
2. Add potatoes, whole chicken thighs and salt to the pot and cook for a further 2 minutes, until fragrant. Add stock and hot water and bring to the boil while stirring. Reduce to a simmer and cook for 15–20 minutes, stirring occasionally, until soup has thickened and chicken is cooked through.
3. Use a slotted spoon or tongs to remove chicken from chowder and roughly chop into bite-sized pieces. Return chicken to pot, along with corn and cream. Stir well and cook for a further 1–2 minutes until corn is cooked. Season to taste with salt and freshly ground black pepper.
4. While corn cooks, place dinner rolls on a baking tray and heat in oven for about 3 minutes, until golden and warmed through.

TO SERVE, spoon chicken chowder into bowls and serve 1–2 dinner rolls on the side, buttered if desired.

ENERGY 2485KJ (594kcal)
CARBS 54.9g
PROTEIN 31.1g
FAT 26.8g

COOK'S HINT

If you want to hide veggies from your little ones, use a stick blender to blitz soup after removing whole chicken thighs.

SERVES 4
PREP TIME 20 minutes
COOK TIME 35 minutes
READY IN 55 minutes

Spiced Pumpkin Filos

Bring these scrummy morsels along to your next dinner party as a tasty vegetarian option.

- 500g pumpkin, peeled and diced 1cm
- 2 carrots, diced 1cm
- ½ red onion, thinly sliced
- ¼ tsp salt
- 1 tbsp sesame seeds
- 1 tbsp filo spice mix (see below)
- 2 tbsp sliced almonds
- ½ cup raisins
- 200g feta cheese, crumbled
- 1–2 handfuls baby spinach leaves
- 10 sheets filo pastry
- 2–3 tbsp melted butter or olive oil
- 2 tbsp sesame seeds

Filo spice mix

Mix together 1 tsp dried thyme, 1 tsp dried marjoram, 1 tsp dried oregano and ½ tsp ground cumin

¼ cup natural yoghurt, relish or sauce, to serve (optional)

PREHEAT oven to 220°C. Line an oven tray with baking paper.

1. Toss pumpkin, carrots, onion, salt, first measure of sesame seeds and filo spice mix with a little oil on prepared tray. Bake for 20–25 minutes, until tender and starting to caramelise.
2. When pumpkin has 5 minutes of cooking time remaining, add almonds, raisins and feta cheese and cook for about 5 minutes, until warmed through. Transfer all to a large bowl and toss through spinach until wilted. Season to taste with salt and freshly ground black pepper and set aside to cool slightly. Line oven tray with a clean sheet of baking paper.
3. Place 1 sheet of filo on a clean, dry bench with a short edge closest to you. Lightly brush with melted butter/oil and fold in half lengthways. Brush folded sheet again with butter/oil.
4. Place ⅓ cup spiced pumpkin filo mixture in the corner of the filo and fold over to form a triangle at the bottom of the sheet. Fold up to form a further triangle and continue folding over until the whole sheet is wrapped around the filling. Repeat with remaining sheets and filling.
5. Place filos on prepared tray and sprinkle with second measure of sesame seeds. Bake for 8–10 minutes, until golden brown. Set aside to cool slightly for about 5 minutes before serving.

TO SERVE, place spiced pumpkin filos on plates with a spoon of yoghurt, relish or sauce on the side (if using).

ENERGY 2190KJ (523kcal)
CARBS 56.3g
PROTEIN 17.9g
FAT 24.3g

WHY NOT TRY?

If you have leftover roast veggies, try using these in the filling instead of pumpkin.

SERVES 4
PREP TIME 15 minutes
COOK TIME 20 minutes
READY IN 35 minutes

Spinach 'n' Cheese Filos

If you don't have frozen spinach, you can swap for 500g fresh spinach — just wilt it down in the pan with the onion and garlic and allow to cool before placing into filos.

- 1 brown onion, finely diced
- 1 clove garlic, minced
- 500g frozen spinach, defrosted
- 200g feta cheese, crumbled
- 1 egg
- ¼ tsp ground nutmeg
- ½ tsp salt
- 8 sheets filo pastry
- 2–3 tbsp melted butter or olive oil (for brushing)
- 1–2 tbsp sesame seeds

- ¼ cup relish or sauce, to serve (optional)

PREHEAT oven to 220°C. Line an oven tray with baking paper.

1. Heat a little olive oil in a medium frying pan on a medium heat. Cook onion for 3 minutes, add garlic and cook for a further 2–3 minutes, until onion is soft. Place spinach in a colander or sieve and use clean hands to push down and squeeze out excess water. Roughly chop spinach.
2. In a large bowl, combine cooked onion and garlic, spinach, feta cheese, egg, nutmeg and salt. Place 1 sheet of filo on a clean, dry bench with short edge closest to you. Lightly brush with butter/oil and fold in half lengthways. Brush folded sheet with butter/oil.
3. Place ¼ cup spinach and cheese mixture in the corner of the filo and fold over to form a triangle at the bottom of the sheet. Fold up to form a further triangle and continue folding over until the whole sheet is wrapped around the filling. Repeat with remaining sheets and filling.
4. Place filos on prepared baking tray, lightly brush with butter/oil and sprinkle with sesame seeds. Bake for 8–10 minutes, until golden brown. Set aside to cool slightly for 5 minutes before serving.

TO SERVE, place spinach 'n' cheese filos onto plates with a dollop of relish or sauce on the side (if using).

ENERGY 1608KJ (384kcal)
CARBS 29.9g
PROTEIN 16.3g
FAT 21.6g

FUN FACT

Filo pastry originated in Turkey and is still used in many Middle Eastern classics — you might also see it called *phyllo* in Greek cookery.

SERVES 4–5
PREP TIME 15 minutes
COOK TIME 30 minutes
READY IN 40 minutes

Chicken Curry Filos

Everyone enjoys the crispy crunch of filo! If you have any left over curry, it'll work great in these — just make sure the curry isn't too saucy.

- 600g boneless, skinless chicken thighs
- 1 brown onion, finely diced
- 1 tbsp curry spice mix (see below)
- 1 cup coconut cream
- 2 tbsp cornflour, mixed with 2 tbsp water
- 1 courgette, grated
- 100g baby spinach leaves
- 2 tbsp soy sauce
- 8–10 sheets filo pastry
- 2–3 tbsp melted butter or olive oil (for brushing)
- 2 tsp sesame seeds

Curry spice mix

Mix together 2 tsp curry powder, 2 tsp garam masala and ½ tsp turmeric

¼ cup chutney, to serve (optional)

PREHEAT oven to 220°C. Line an oven tray with baking paper.

1. Heat a little oil in a large frying pan on a high heat. Pat chicken dry with paper towels and season with salt and freshly ground black pepper. Cook chicken for about 2 minutes each side, until golden. Add onion and curry spice mix and cook for about 3 minutes, until onion has softened.
2. Reduce heat to medium and add coconut cream. Bring to a simmer and cook for about 3 minutes, until chicken is cooked through. Add cornflour mixture, courgette and spinach to pan and cook for about 2 minutes, until veggies are tender and sauce has thickened. Remove from heat, stir through soy sauce and shred chicken in pan using two forks. Season to taste with salt and freshly ground black pepper.
3. Place 1 sheet of filo on a clean, dry bench with a short edge closest to you. Lightly brush with melted butter/oil and place another sheet of filo on top. Brush again with melted butter/oil and fold in half lengthways. Brush folded sheet with melted butter or oil.
4. Divide chicken curry mixture into 4–5 portions (about 1 cup each) and place in the corner of the filo. Fold over to form a triangle at the bottom of the sheet. Fold up to form a further triangle and continue folding over until the whole sheet is wrapped around filling. Repeat with remaining sheets and filling.
5. Place filos on prepared baking tray, lightly brush with melted butter/oil and sprinkle with sesame seeds. Bake for 8–10 minutes, until golden brown. Set aside to cool slightly for 5 minutes before serving.

TO SERVE, place chicken curry filos on plates and serve chutney (if using) on the side.

ENERGY 2639KJ (631kcal)
CARBS 33.6g
PROTEIN 32.0g
FAT 41.1g

VEGGIE
DELIGHT

SERVES 2–3
PREP TIME 15 minutes
COOK TIME 15 minutes
READY IN 30 minutes

- 2 cups frozen corn kernels
- 1 cup flour
- 1 tsp baking powder
- ½ tsp salt
- ½ tsp ground cumin
- 3 eggs, lightly beaten
- ⅓ cup milk
- ¼ cup chopped parsley, leaves and stalks (or 1 tsp dried parsley)
- 2–3 tbsp oil

To serve

- ½ cup sour cream
- 1½–2 tbsp sweet chilli sauce (preferably mild)
- 1 lemon, cut into wedges, to serve (optional)

Corn Fritters

These fritters are great to throw in kids lunch boxes or for a Saturday afternoon treat.

BRING a medium-sized pot of salted water to the boil.

1. Cook corn in pot of boiling water for 1–2 minutes. Drain, refresh under cold water, then drain again. Set aside.
2. In a large bowl, whisk flour, baking powder, salt, cumin, eggs and milk together until smooth. Season with freshly ground black pepper. Fold through parsley and corn. Set aside for 10 minutes.
3. Heat oil in a large frying pan on a medium heat. Place spoonfuls of mixture into pan and cook, in batches, for 1–2 minutes each side, or until golden. Drain on paper towels. Add more oil between batches, if needed.
4. Mix sour cream and sweet chilli sauce together in a small bowl, until combined (if using).

TO SERVE, place a few corn fritters onto each plate and top with a dollop of sweet chilli sour cream. Serve with a wedge of lemon to squeeze over just before eating (if using).

ENERGY 2178KJ (521kcal)
CARBS 61.3g
PROTEIN 18.5g
FAT 21.4g

COOK'S HINT

Swap the parsely in the fritter batter for your favourite fresh herb.

SERVES 4
PREP TIME 20 minutes
COOK TIME 40 minutes
READY IN 45 minutes

Ham 'n' Cheese Quiche with Roast Pumpkin Salad

This quiche makes the perfect picnic lunch — eat it hot or cold and enjoy with friends.

Ham 'n' cheese quiche

- 1½ cups flour
- 1 tsp baking powder
- 3½ tbsp butter, softened (but not melted)
- ½ cup water
- ½ brown onion
- 200g ham
- 1 courgette
- 1 cup grated cheese
- ½ tsp salt
- 4 eggs (at room temperature)
- ¾ cup milk
- 1 tomato, thinly sliced

Roast pumpkin salad

- 400g pumpkin, peeled
- 1 carrot
- 1 tbsp oil
- 2 tomatoes
- 1 capsicum
- ½ iceberg lettuce
- 1–2 tbsp olive oil
- 1–2 tbsp vinegar (e.g. red wine, white wine, white, cider)

PREHEAT oven to 230°C. Line an oven tray with baking paper. Grease a large casserole dish (measuring about 20cm x 30cm) or a large round quiche dish with oil.

1. Sift flour and baking powder together in a large bowl. Using clean, dry hands rub butter into flour (or use a food processer to combine), until it resembles breadcrumbs. Add water, gently mix into a dough with a butter knife and, once combined, form a ball with your hands.
2. Using clean, dry hands, spread dough (about 3mm thick) across base and sides (3–4cm high) of casserole dish. Place in oven for 5 minutes, while you prepare the filling.
3. Finely dice onion; roughly chop ham; grate courgette and squeeze out excess moisture with a tea towel. Remove casserole dish from oven and carefully layer first ham, then onion, courgette and ¾ cup cheese into dish and sprinkle with salt.
4. Crack eggs into a bowl, whisk lightly then add milk. Season with freshly ground black pepper and whisk to combine. Pour mixture over quiche filling and top with sliced tomato and remaining cheese. Bake for about 35 minutes, until golden brown and filling has set. Set aside to cool for 5 minutes.
5. While quiche cooks, dice pumpkin and carrot into 1cm pieces and toss on prepared tray with oil. Roast for 25–30 minutes, until cooked through. Allow to cool slightly before adding to salad.
6. While quiche and pumpkin are cooking, prepare remainder of salad. Dice tomatoes into 1cm pieces; remove core and seeds and finely slice capsicum; roughly chop lettuce. Place all in a large bowl along with cooked pumpkin and carrot. Add oil and vinegar, mix to combine and season to taste with salt and freshly ground black pepper.

TO SERVE, slice ham 'n' cheese quiche into squares, place onto plates and serve salad on the side.

ENERGY 2594KJ (620kcal)
CARBS 49.5g
PROTEIN 32.1g
FAT 31.6g

SERVES 5
PREP TIME 15 minutes
COOK TIME 35 minutes
READY IN 45 minutes

Bacon 'n' Egg Frittata

Derived from the omelette, frittata is an Italian word roughly translating to 'fried'.

Bacon and egg frittata

800g potatoes, scrubbed and diced 1.5cm
300g bacon, thinly sliced
1 brown onion, thinly sliced
250g frozen corn kernels, defrosted
2–3 handfuls baby spinach leaves
6 eggs (at room temperature)
½ cup milk
1 tsp salt
½ cup grated cheese

Salad

1 capsicum
½ iceberg lettuce
½ telegraph cucumber
1–2 tbsp olive oil (optional)
1–2 tbsp vinegar (e.g. red wine, white wine, white, cider; optional)

tomato sauce, to serve (optional)

PREHEAT oven to 200°C. Bring a medium-sized pot of salted water to the boil. Grease a large casserole dish (measuring about 20cm x 30cm).

1. Cook potatoes in pot of boiling water for about 10 minutes, until just cooked. Drain well and set aside.
2. Heat a little oil in a large frying pan on a medium-high heat. Cook bacon for 3–4 minutes, until starting to become crispy. Add onion and cook for a further 3–4 minutes, until softened. Stir through corn and spinach and remove from heat.
3. Toss potatoes through bacon mixture and add to greased dish. Spread out evenly to cover the base.
4. In a medium-sized bowl, whisk eggs, milk and salt together and season with freshly ground black pepper. Gently pour over top of bacon/potatoes then shake dish to distribute mixture. Top with cheese. Bake for 20–25 minutes, until set. Turn dish once during cooking. Once cooked, allow to rest for 5–10 minutes.
5. While frittata is cooking, prepare salad. Remove core and seeds from capsicum. Thinly slice capsicum, lettuce and cucumber. Toss all in a medium-sized bowl with olive oil and vinegar (if using) and season to taste with salt and freshly ground black pepper.

TO SERVE, cut bacon and egg frittata into pieces and divide among plates. Serve salad and tomato sauce on the side (if using).

WHY NOT TRY?

A frittata is a great dish to use up any remaining ingredients in your fridge at the end of the week. You could use pumpkin, kumara, carrots, corn, courgette — the options are limitless.

ENERGY 2285KJ (546kcal)
CARBS 49.9g
PROTEIN 37.7g
FAT 21.0g

MAKE AHEAD

SERVES 4
PREP TIME 20 minutes
COOK TIME 35 minutes
READY IN 45 minutes

Bacon 'n' Egg Pie with Orange Salad

Another Kiwi classic — you won't have to pop to the bakery for this one ever again!

Orange salad

- 200g pumpkin, peeled and diced 1cm
- 3 stalks celery
- 2–3 handfuls baby spinach leaves
- 1 spring onion, green part only
- 2 oranges
- 2 tbsp olive oil
- 1 tsp vinegar (e.g. red wine, white wine)

Bacon 'n' egg pie

- 1 sheet flaky puff pastry (about 350g)
- 300g shoulder bacon, rind removed and diced 2–3cm
- ½ brown onion, finely diced
- 1 spring onion, finely diced
- 4 eggs

- 3–4 tbsp tomato sauce, to serve (optional)

PREHEAT oven to 220°C. Line two oven trays with baking paper.

1. Toss pumpkin with a little oil on first prepared tray and season with salt and freshly ground black pepper. Place in oven (on the bottom rack) and roast for 15–18 minutes, until softened and golden. Turn once during cooking. Once cooked, remove from oven and set aside to cool.
2. While pumpkin cooks, place pastry onto second prepared tray (some pastry will be hanging off the side). Lay bacon evenly onto left half of pastry, leaving a 1cm border around the edge (there will be several layers of bacon).
3. Top bacon with diced onion and spring onion in an even layer. Create four indents in the pie filling, big enough to crack eggs into (until you can see bare pastry at the bottom of each indent). Crack eggs into indents, being careful not to let egg run, and gently break yolks with a fork. Season with salt and freshly ground black pepper.
4. Gently dip a pastry brush into the yolk and brush around the border of the pastry. Pull the unfilled side of pastry over the filling so all edges meet, pressing down on edges firmly. Use a fork to press the three open edges together, making sure they seal. Make a couple of small slits in the top of the pie with a sharp knife to allow steam to escape.
5. Place in oven (on rack above pumpkin) and bake for 20–25 minutes, until pastry is golden. Set aside to rest for 5 minutes before slicing.
6. While pie rests, prepare the rest of the salad. Thinly slice celery on an angle; roughly chop spinach; thinly slice spring onion; peel oranges and dice into 1cm pieces. Place all in a medium-sized bowl along with cooled pumpkin. Add oil and vinegar and toss gently to combine. Season to taste with salt and freshly ground black pepper.

TO SERVE, place a piece of bacon 'n' egg pie onto each plate. Top with tomato sauce (if using) and spoon some orange salad on the side.

ENERGY 2439KJ (583kcal)
CARBS 42.1g
PROTEIN 23.3g
FAT 35.2g

SWEET AS

BARGAIN BOX is all about creating wholesome, tasty meals the whole family will love. Still, we reckon no cookbook is *truly* complete without any meal's crowning glory . . . dessert! For this section we've gathered recipes for irresistible desserts and baked treats — puddings, lunchbox ideas — and an easy-as, real fruit ice cream. Perfect for getting your little chefs involved in the kitchen, whether they're whipping up bananas or shaping bikkies, they're sure to learn a thing or two. Oh, and don't miss the absolute knockout chocolate pudding!

KID
APPROVED

SERVES 4
PREP TIME 10 minutes
COOK TIME 30 minutes
READY IN 35 minutes

Feijoa Crumble

There couldn't be a more heartwarming dish than a cinnamon-spiced crumble on a cold winter's eve. Feijoas give this dish great bite.

Filling

- 6 feijoas, flesh scooped out and roughly chopped
- 2 apples, peeled and diced 2cm
- 2 tbsp brown sugar
- ¼ cup water

Crumble topping

- ¼ cup plain flour
- ½ cup rolled oats
- ¼ cup brown sugar
- ¼ cup desiccated coconut or thread coconut
- ¼ cup chopped nuts
- ½ tsp ground cinnamon
- ½ tsp vanilla essence
- 30g chilled butter, diced 1cm

- ½ cup natural yoghurt, to serve (optional)

PREHEAT oven to 200°C.

1. Place all filling ingredients in a medium-sized pot and bring to the boil. As soon as it boils, reduce heat to medium and simmer for 5 minutes, until tender. Drain off any excess liquid and transfer feijoas and apples to a medium-sized oven-proof dish.
2. Place all crumble topping ingredients in a medium-sized bowl. Use your fingers to rub ingredients together, until mixture resembles breadcrumbs.
3. Sprinkle crumble topping over stewed fruit and bake for 15–20 minutes, until topping is golden.

TO SERVE, spoon crumble into bowls and serve with yoghurt (if using).

ENERGY 1257KJ (300kcal)
CARBS 33.9g
PROTEIN 5.2g
FAT 14.9g

WHY NOT TRY?

You can substitute feijoas with any in-season fruit, such as apples, apricots, pears or even tamarillos.

SERVES 10
PREP TIME 15 minutes
COOK TIME 55 minutes
READY IN 60 minutes

Sticky Date Pudding with Butterscotch Sauce

The *pièce de résistance* of all our desserts, this pudding is so completely irresistible it will have you licking the bowl!

Sticky date pudding

2½ cups pitted dried dates
1 cup water
1 tsp baking soda
4 tbsp butter
2 eggs
⅓ cup white sugar (preferably caster sugar)
½ tsp salt
1 tsp vanilla essence
1½ cups plain flour
1½ tbsp baking powder

Butterscotch sauce

150g butter
¾ cup cream
1 cup brown sugar

vanilla ice cream or runny cream, to serve (optional)

PREHEAT oven to 170°C. Grease an oven-proof dish (measuring about 20cm x 20cm) with butter.

1. Place dates and water in a medium-sized pot on a medium-high heat. Cook for about 6 minutes, stirring often, until dates are soft, have broken down and water has evaporated. Remove from heat and stir through baking soda and butter, until combined and butter is melted. Set aside for about 10 minutes to cool slightly.
2. While date mixture is cooling, lightly whisk eggs in a large bowl. Place cooled date mixture into bowl with eggs and add sugar, salt and vanilla essence. Stir until combined, then sift in flour and baking powder. Gently fold through, until just combined.
3. Transfer mixture into prepared dish and bake for about 45 minutes, until golden and a skewer inserted into the middle comes out clean. Set aside for about 5 minutes.
4. When pudding has 5 minutes of cooking time remaining, prepare butterscotch sauce. Combine all butterscotch sauce ingredients in a small pot on a medium heat. Bring sauce to a gentle simmer, then reduce heat to low to cook for a further 3–4 minutes, until sugar has dissolved and sauce has thickened slightly.
5. Poke about 15 holes in the top of the pudding using the end of a spoon or a skewer. Pour over half the butterscotch sauce (reserving half to serve) and leave for about 1 minute to soak into the pudding slightly.

TO SERVE, cut sticky date pudding into squares and serve on plates or in bowls, pouring over remaining butterscotch sauce (if desired). Serve ice cream on the side, or drizzle over runny cream (if using).

ENERGY 2238KJ (535kcal)
CARBS 68.0g
PROTEIN 5.5g
FAT 26.1g

READY
IN 10

SERVES 4
PREP TIME 10 minutes

Easy Ice Cream

For when you're craving something sweet but don't want to go to the shop, this is a quick and easy homemade dessert.

- 500g frozen berries (e.g. blueberries, strawberries, raspberries, boysenberries)
- 100ml cream
- 1–2 tbsp runny honey (optional)

1. Place berries into food processor and blend, while drizzling in cream. Blend until mixture is smooth and the consistency of ice cream.
2. Add honey (if using) and blitz briefly to combine.

SERVE the ice cream immediately, or scoop into a container and store in the freezer until ready to serve.

ENERGY 687KJ (164kcal)
CARBS 15.2g
PROTEIN 0.5g
FAT 10.0g

COOK'S HINT

You can use any of your favourite fruity flavours in this recipe. If you can't find the frozen fruit you want at the store, try dicing fresh fruit into bite-sized pieces and freezing them overnight — mango, feijoa, nectarine or plum are all great options. Add some extra flavour to your ice cream with fresh mint or vanilla, and you could even top with some chopped nuts for added texture. Yum!

YUM!

SERVES 6
PREP TIME 10 minutes
COOK TIME 30 minutes
READY IN 40 minutes

Chocolate Self-Saucing Pudding

A truly decadent, yet simple and affordable, dessert.

½ cup milk
1 egg
115g butter, melted
1 cup plain flour
1 tsp baking powder
2 tbsp cocoa powder
½ cup brown sugar
¾ cup brown sugar
2 tbsp cocoa powder
1¼ cups boiling water

To serve

1 tbsp icing sugar
1 cup cream, whipped (optional)
1 cup frozen berries, defrosted (optional)

PREHEAT oven to 180°C. Grease a medium baking dish (measuring about 20cm x 15cm). Bring a full kettle to the boil.

1. In a medium-sized bowl, whisk together milk, egg and melted butter.
2. Into a large bowl, sift flour, baking powder and first measure of cocoa, then stir in first measure of brown sugar.
3. Slowly add the milk mixture to the flour mixture, whisking gently until smooth and combined. Pour into prepared dish and smooth into an even layer with a spoon or spatula.
4. Put second measure of brown sugar in a small bowl and sift in second measure of cocoa. Stir to combine then sprinkle evenly over pudding.
5. Slowly pour boiling water onto the back of a large metal spoon over the pudding, to cover evenly. Place baking dish on a baking tray, to prevent any spills while baking.
6. Bake for 25–30 minutes, or until pudding bounces back when pressed gently in centre. Serve immediately.

TO SERVE, dust with icing sugar and serve with whipped cream (if using) and your favourite frozen berries (if using).

ENERGY 2101KJ (502kcal)
CARBS 50.4g
PROTEIN 6.1g
FAT 30.8g

MIX IT UP

Add some cinnamon to the topping for an extra pop of flavour.

WINTER
WARMER

SERVES 4
PREP TIME 5 minutes
COOK TIME 35 minutes
READY IN 30 minutes

Creamy Rice Pudding

Rice pudding is such an easy and versatile base for a dessert. This is a simple recipe to get you started, but it'll be great with any of your favourite treats added in!

1 cup jasmine rice
1½ cups water
pinch of salt
1 cup coconut milk, plus extra to serve
¾ cup milk
1 tsp vanilla essence
1½ tbsp runny honey

To serve

1–2 pears, cored
pinch of ground cinnamon (optional)

1. Combine rice, water and salt in a medium-sized lidded pot and bring to the boil. As soon as it boils, cover with a tight-fitting lid and reduce to lowest heat to cook for 12 minutes. Turn off heat and leave to steam, still covered, for a further 8 minutes. Do not lift lid during cooking or steaming.
2. Mix together 2 cups cooked rice, coconut milk, milk and vanilla essence in a small pot and simmer on a medium heat, stirring frequently (to avoid it burning on the bottom), for 6–8 minutes, until thick and creamy. Reduce heat if pudding starts to stick.
3. While rice pudding is cooking, cut pear into thin slices.
4. Stir honey through cooked rice pudding.

TO SERVE, spoon rice pudding into bowls, drizzle with extra coconut milk and top with slices of pear and a pinch of ground cinnamon, (if using).

ENERGY 1485KJ (355kcal)
CARBS 55.4g
PROTEIN 5.6g
FAT 12.6g

FUN FACT

Different variations of rice pudding are eaten all over the world, particularly in Asia and India where rice is a staple. There's baked rice, coconut rice, rice in the slow-cooker, rice with cream, fruit or nuts! Try your hand at a few different combinations.

SERVES 8
PREP TIME 5–10 minutes
+ freezing time

Troppo Pops

A quick, easy and healthy snack for your little ones to enjoy in summer.

425g fresh or canned pineapple
165ml coconut cream
½ cup natural yoghurt
1 tsp vanilla essence
2 tbsp runny honey

1. Blend all ingredients together in a blender or food processor until smooth.
2. Pour into 8 ice-block moulds and freeze until hard.

ENERGY 399KJ (95kcal)
CARBS 11.3g
PROTEIN 1.1g
FAT 5.2g

WHY NOT TRY?

For the adults, freeze this mixture into ice cubes and blend up for a smoothie — or even a cheeky cocktail!

MAKES 20
PREP TIME 15 minutes
COOK TIME 15 minutes
READY IN 30 minutes

Anzac Biscuits

Who doesn't love an Anzac biscuit? This one is perfect for dunking in your tea or packing into school lunches.

1 cup rolled oats
¾ cup desiccated coconut
1 cup wholemeal flour
¾ cup sugar
125g butter, diced 1cm
1 tbsp golden syrup or runny honey
1 tsp baking soda
5 tbsp boiling water

PREHEAT oven to 180°C. Bring a half-full kettle to the boil. Line two oven trays with baking paper.

1. Place oats, coconut, flour and sugar into a large bowl.
2. Combine butter and golden syrup/honey in a small pot on a low-medium heat and stir until melted. In a small dish, mix baking soda and boiling water together until baking soda has dissolved. Stir baking soda mixture into butter mixture.
3. Stir butter mixture through dry ingredients until well combined. Use damp hands to roll tablespoons of mixture into about 20 balls. Place on prepared trays, 5cm apart. Flatten to 5mm with a damp fork.
4. Bake biscuits for 8–10 minutes, until golden brown. Swap trays halfway through to ensure even cooking. Remove from oven and cool on trays. The biscuits will firm up as they cool. Remove from trays to completely cool on a rack. If you prefer a crunchier biscuit, cook for 3–4 more minutes.
5. Serve immediately or store in an airtight container.

ENERGY 578KJ (138kcal)
CARBS 14.8g
PROTEIN 1.6g
FAT 7.9g

DID YOU KNOW?

Anzac biscuits were first made to send to Australian and New Zealand soldiers fighting in World War I. Because the ingredients didn't spoil, the biscuits kept well on the long trip to the battlegrounds.

MAKES 1 loaf
SERVES 10
PREP TIME 15 minutes
COOK TIME 45–50 minutes
READY IN 65 minutes

Bangin' Banana Bread

Everybody's favourite afternoon tea, smear a scrummy slice of this banana bread with butter and serve with a good cuppa!

125g softened butter
1 cup brown sugar
2 eggs
1½ cups plain flour
1 tsp baking powder
1 tsp baking soda
¼ cup natural yoghurt
¼ cup milk
2 ripe bananas, mashed

PREHEAT oven to 180°C. Grease a loaf tin (measuring about 22cm x 15 cm) and line with baking paper.

1. In a large bowl, use an electric mixer to beat butter and sugar until pale and creamy. Add eggs, beating well to combine.
2. Sift flour, baking powder and baking soda into the butter mixture. Stir until well combined.
3. In a small bowl, whisk yoghurt and milk together. Add yoghurt mixture and bananas to flour mixture and mix well.
4. Spoon mixture into prepared loaf tin. Bake for 45–50 minutes, until a skewer inserted into centre comes out clean. Allow to cool for 5–10 minutes before turning out onto a wire rack to cool completely.

TO SERVE, cut into slices and divide between plates.

ENERGY 1093KJ (261kcal)
CARBS 34.3g
PROTEIN 4.2g
FAT 12.1g

COOK'S HINT

Although this bread is sweet enough on its own, the addition of chocolate chips is always a welcome treat.

The Bargain Box Pantry

Keep a selection of these dried herbs and spices in your pantry to experiment with in your cooking. You can store leftover spice mixes in airtight containers or sealable bags.

CAYENNE PEPPER

Cayenne pepper is often used in Mexican, Italian and Indian dishes, and is great paired with eggs and cheese. It will add heat to your dish without changing the flavour profile. Just remember — you only need a small pinch as it's very spicy!

CHILLI POWDER

Chilli powder is made from dried and ground chillis, and is most popular in Mexican and Cajun-style dishes. Just a small amount adds spiciness to meals, so use with caution.

CORIANDER FLAKES

Not to be confused with ground coriander, coriander flakes are the dried leaves of the coriander plant. They have a mild, aromatic flavour and are often used in Asian, Indian and Mexican dishes.

CURRY POWDER

Curry powder is another popular blend of ground spices used in a variety of dishes and cuisines. Common ingredients include coriander, turmeric, cumin, ginger and cayenne pepper. This blend is perfect for a Kiwi fav, curried eggs!

DRIED BASIL

Dried basil has hints of aniseed, but is a lot milder than fresh basil. It is most commonly used in Italian cooking, as it pairs perfectly with tomatoes and cheese.

DRIED MARJORAM

Dried marjoram is similar to dried oregano, but has a citrusy aroma and a slightly milder and sweeter flavour. It is often used in French and British cooking, and is delicious with meat and root vegetables.

DRIED MINT

Dried mint is warm and aromatic, with a refreshing aftertaste. It is ideal for lamb and fish dishes, and in sauces, jellies and chutneys.

DRIED OREGANO

Dried oregano is commonly used in Greek, Italian, Middle Eastern and Mexican cuisines. It is warm and aromatic, with a slight bitterness, and is often used on pizzas and in tomato-based sauces.

DRIED PARSLEY

Dried parsley has a subtle, fresh flavour that makes it ideal for use in many dishes, including soups, stews and stuffings. It also goes well with most proteins including chicken, eggs and fish. This versatile herb is a must-have in your pantry!

DRIED ROSEMARY

Dried rosemary has a strong, bitter, pine-like flavour and is perfect for pairing with ingredients such as garlic, tomato, red wine and red meats. In NZ, we often pair it with lamb — a perfect combo on the barbecue!

DRIED SAGE

Dried sage is very aromatic and has a slight peppery flavour. Here in New Zealand, we often use it in stuffings for roast chicken, pork or turkey. Dried sage is also perfect in slow-cooked meals, as it doesn't lose its flavour during cooking.

GARAM MASALA

Garam masala is a blend of ground spices commonly used in Indian and Pakistani cuisine. Common ingredients include nutmeg, cardamom, nutmeg, cayenne and black pepper, cinnamon, coriander, cumin, star anise, fennel, clove and garlic. Garam masala is often used for a deeper flavour in curries and casseroles, and even in baking.

GARLIC POWDER

Made from dehydrated and ground garlic cloves, garlic powder is slightly sweet and has a milder flavour than fresh garlic. It works well with ingredients such as ginger, lemongrass and chilli.

GROUND CARDAMOM

This warm and aromatic spice is widely used in Indian cuisine, including in garam masala. Made from the ground seeds of the cardamom plant, ground cardamom is often used in desserts and baking, including rice puddings, fruit cakes and biscuits.

GROUND CLOVES

Cloves (whole and ground) are an important ingredient in garam masala, as well as in Chinese five spice. Ground cloves are commonly used in curries, stewed fruits, pickles and baking. This spice is extremely strong and aromatic so should only be used in small amounts!

GROUND CORIANDER

Ground coriander is made from the dried, ground seeds of the coriander plant, and has a lemony citrus flavour. Often found in Indian curries, you will also find whole seeds in some pickling liquids.

GROUND CUMIN

Cumin seeds (whole and ground) are widely used in many cuisines, from Indian curries to Mexican and Moroccan spice mixes. The seeds have a distinctive flavour and aroma, and you may have even tried them in some cheeses — look out for cumin gouda at your supermarket, it's delicious!

GROUND GINGER

Ground ginger is made from fresh ginger root that has been dried and ground. It is slightly sharper in flavour than fresh ginger and is common in baking and desserts, smoothies and other breakfast foods.

GROUND TURMERIC

Made from fresh turmeric that has been dried and ground, ground turmeric has a deep orange-yellow colour that will stain anything (so use with care)! It is commonly used for colour and flavour in South East Asian cuisine.

LEMON PEPPER

Lemon pepper is a spice blend containing — you guessed it — lemon and pepper! It is commonly used in chicken, fish and rice dishes, and adds a touch of spice and tanginess to your meals.

ONION POWDER

Onion powder is dehydrated, ground onion, with a warm, sweet and salty flavour. It can be used as a seasoning in many dishes including pasta, pizza, burger patties, sauces, soups and meat rubs.

SMOKED PAPRIKA

Smoked paprika is made from capsicums that have been dried over a wood fire, giving it a rich, earthy, smoky flavour. It has a vibrant red colour, and is popular in Spanish cuisine.

Tasty Toppings

A collection of some of our favourites for you to keep on hand.

Tartare Sauce

MAKES ½ cup PREP TIME 5 minutes

1 tbsp chopped capers
2½ tbsp chopped gherkins
¼ cup mayo
zest and juice of 1 lemon

COMBINE all ingredients in a small bowl.

Basil Pesto

MAKES 1 cup COOK TIME 5 minutes
PREP TIME 5 minutes READY IN 10 minutes

¼ cup pine nuts or cashew nuts
1½ cups packed basil leaves
½ cup packed parsley leaves and stalks
½ clove garlic, finely chopped
¼ cup grated Parmesan cheese
⅓ cup olive oil
1–2 tbsp lemon juice

1. Heat a small, dry, frying pan on a medium heat. Toast pine nuts/cashews for about 30 seconds, until light brown. Remove from pan and cool slightly.
2. Place nuts, basil leaves, parsley, garlic and Parmesan in a food processor and blitz to combine, while slowly drizzling in olive oil.
3. Season to taste with lemon juice, salt and freshly ground black pepper. Pesto will keep in the fridge for a few days or can be frozen in a sealable bag for a few months.

Thai Dressing

MAKES ½ cup PREP TIME 5 minutes

juice of 1 lime
2 tbsp sweet chilli sauce (preferably mild)
2 tbsp fish sauce
2 tbsp water
1 clove garlic, minced

COMBINE all ingredients in a small bowl.

COOK'S HINT

Store extra dressing in an airtight container or jar for up to 1 week.

Honey Soy Dressing

MAKES 1 cup PREP TIME 5 minutes

4 tbsp soy sauce
2 tbsp Worcestershire sauce
3 tbsp brown sugar
1 tbsp honey
4 tbsp sesame oil
2 tbsp finely grated ginger

COMBINE all ingredients in a small bowl.

COOK'S HINT

Store extra dressing in an airtight container or jar for up to 1 week.

Homemade Pizza Dough

MAKES 4 bases

1 cup lukewarm water
1 tbsp active dried yeast
1 tsp sugar
450g high-grade flour
1 tbsp olive oil
1 tsp salt

1. Put water in a bowl and add the yeast and sugar. Stir gently and leave in a warm place until the yeast has dissolved and the mixture is very frothy. Mix well.
2. Place flour, olive oil and salt in a large mixing bowl. Add the yeast mixture and mix well to form a dough (note: there may be some leftover flour in the bowl once you've formed the dough, this is fine).
3. Knead the dough for 8–10 minutes until smooth and elastic (when you push in a finger the dough should bounce back), then place in an oiled bowl. Cover with a tea towel or cling film and leave in a warm place to rise until double in size (this will take about 40 minutes).
4. Once the dough has risen, knock it back by punching it with your fist (to knock out some of the air), then cut it into 4 pieces. Roll out each pizza base on a floured surface into a roughly shaped disc, about 20cm in diameter (they should be nice and thin to help them go crispy). Your pizza bases are now ready to use!

Index

Special thanks to the Bargain Box Kitchen development team and our little chefs – Angus, Holly, Immie, Hattie, Natalya, Noah, Paige and Yaan. Thanks also to Factory Ceramics of Waiheke Island, Source and Home, Freedom and Città for supplying props.

RANDOM HOUSE

UK | USA | Canada | Ireland | Australia
India | New Zealand | South Africa | China

Random House is an imprint of the Penguin Random House group of companies, whose addresses can be found at global.penguinrandomhouse.com.

First published by Penguin Random House New Zealand, 2018

5 7 9 10 8 6

Styling by Victoria Bell

Design by Rachel Clark
© Penguin Random House New Zealand
Prepress by Image Centre Group
Printed and bound in China by Leo Paper Products Ltd

A catalogue record for this book is available from the National Library of New Zealand.

ISBN 978-0-14-377189-0

penguin.co.nz

FSC
www.fsc.org
MIX
Paper from responsible sources
FSC® C020056

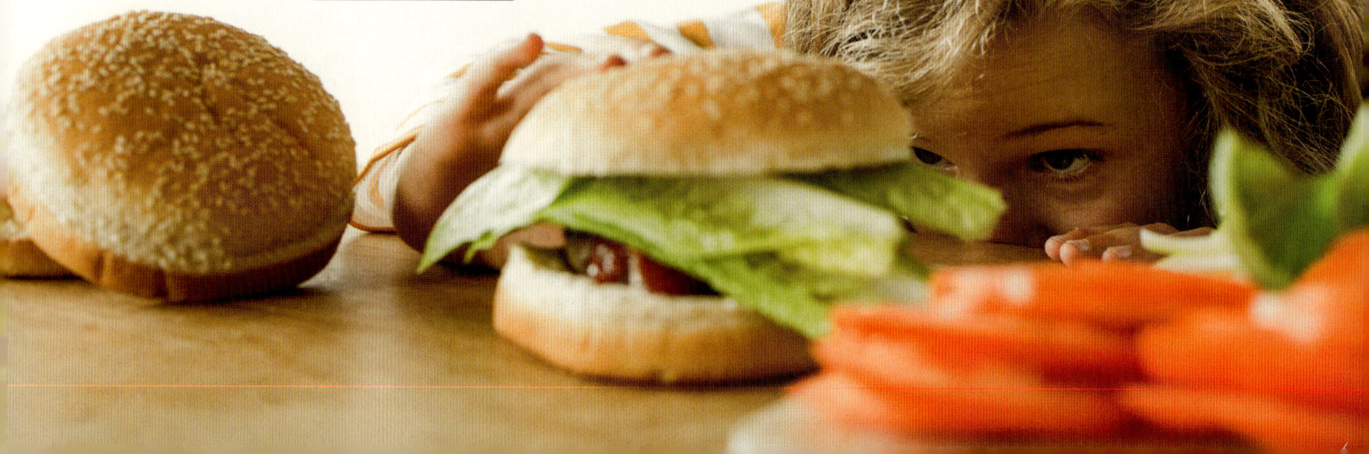